THE YOGA WAY TO RELEASE TENSION

*the text of this book is printed
on 100% recycled paper*

D1043015

OTHER BOOKS BY RACHEL CARR

STEPPING STONES TO JAPANESE FLORAL ART
A YEAR OF FLOWERS
HOURS AND FLOWERS
JAPANESE FLORAL ART: SYMBOLISM, CULT AND PRACTICE
THE JAPANESE WAY WITH FLOWERS
CREATIVE WAYS WITH FLOWERS: THE BEST OF TWO WORLDS,
    EAST AND WEST
THE PICTURE STORY OF JAPAN
YOGA FOR ALL AGES
BE A FROG, A BIRD, OR A TREE (CREATIVE YOGA EXERCISES FOR
    CHILDREN)
YOGA . . . TODAY! (RECORD ALBUM)

THE YOGA WAY TO RELEASE TENSION

Techniques for Relaxation and Mind Control

RACHEL CARR

Illustrated by Lee Eriquezzo

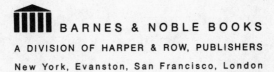

BARNES & NOBLE BOOKS

A DIVISION OF HARPER & ROW, PUBLISHERS

New York, Evanston, San Francisco, London

For Ed, Alain, Kerry, and Chris

Acknowledgments

My special thanks to Dr. Dorothea Kerr, a practicing psychiatrist in New York City, for her comments on this book. Apart from her private practice, Dr. Kerr is an attending psychiatrist at the New York Hospital-Cornell Medical Center.

I am indebted to Dr. Richard Stone and his wife, Doris, for reading the manuscript and for their helpful suggestions. Dr. Stone is the Medical Director-Research of American Telephone and Telegraph Company.

My appreciation is also extended to Dr. Richard Brower, Associate Professor of Biological Science, Manhattan Community College, who checked the accuracy of biomedical information in the text. Dr. Brower was my professor in the study of anatomy and physiology.

My thanks to Dr. George S. Stevenson for permission to quote from his booklet *How to Deal With Your Tensions*, published by the National Association for Mental Health, and to Dr. Elmer Green of the Menninger Foundation for permission to quote from his papers describing his experiments in biofeedback.

I am grateful to Dorothy and Henry Boettinger, who read the text critically.

My deepest appreciation goes to my husband, Ed Kimball, for reading and rereading the manuscript, which added immensely to the clarity of this book.

Contents

Deep-Breathing Exercises

Relaxation, Mind-Control Exercises, and Meditation

EXERCISES FOR DIFFERENT PARTS OF THE BODY

9

FOREWORD

The value of this book goes beyond the realm of physical exercise. It is designed to help you relax and release tension caused by daily pressures. By taking snatches of time from a crowded day for some stretching, toning, deep breathing, and relaxation, you *can* maintain an adequate level of physical fitness.

There is no daily plan to follow, since these yoga-based exercises respond to a specific need: ways to relieve tension headaches, tired eyes, pain in the lower back, stiff neck, aching feet, fatigue, and muscle tension and how to recharge your energy. They work on a subtle interplay of muscles in dynamic action, causing no perspiration or sudden loss of breath control.

You do some of the spot exercises while you are standing, others while you are sitting in a chair, which make them easy to tackle in spare moments in an office. You don't have to wear a gym suit, skip rope, jog, or put up an exercise bar that will turn your office into a health club. You have only to loosen anything that is binding around the neck and waist and at times remove your shoes.

Apart from the spot exercises, a selection of twelve yogic exercises is given to be done at home. These are designed to increase your stamina and endurance and to keep your muscles well toned and your joints limber. You will find them helpful when sustained muscular action is required, as in any sport: golf, tennis, swimming, handball, or even jogging. In the practice of yoga, these are the ones recommended to stimulate sexual activity and to increase freedom of physical expression.

The deep-breathing exercises and those on mind control and body relaxation given in this book can work wonders on your general physical and mental condition. They provide a natural way to stay vibrant and healthy.

Learning to experience moments of internal retreat will give you the ability to relax at will. The deep-breathing and mind-control exercises can be used effectively as tranquilizers and antidepressants, and are especially helpful for "afterbirth blues" in a woman's postpartum period, and for the menopausal stage in her later life when estrogen deficiency brings about depression, anxiety, irritability, nervousness, and even hostility. When the body and mind function like a running stream—smooth and flowing

11

—our endocrine glands are stimulated, increasing the desire for a more responsive sexual life. When that wonderful feeling of being physically fit takes hold, it will make you think of the words of the old spiritual: "When it hits you, you'll holler, yes, indeed!"

Some of the great athletes of our time have turned to serious training in yoga to improve their stamina and ability to relax —Olympic swimmer Mark Spitz, Olympic skier Jean-Claude Killy, golfer Gary Player, world champion deep-sea diver Jacques Mayol, and former middle-weight champion Sugar Ray Robinson. This ancient Indian science of physical and mental health has also reached into the lives of other famous personalities with diverse backgrounds, such as violinist Yehudi Menuhin, conductor Herbert von Karajan, dress designer Pauline Trigère, dancer Ruth St. Denis, opera singer Robert Merrill, ageless movie stars Gloria Swanson and Cary Grant, and the late David Ben-Gurion.

My introduction to yoga was my salvation. The osteoarthritis that I developed in China during the Second World War had forced me for many painful years to sleep on a board with forty pounds of weight pulling on my spine. My entire life was changed when I embarked on a serious study and practice of yoga. In less than six months I was able to discard the traction and board. Through the gentle persuasion of exercising the stiff, unused muscles in my back, I was finally freed of the agony of tension that created chronic muscle spasms. My spine became limber and my figure lithe. There was a bounce in my step.

"You look great!" my friends remarked. "What have you done to yourself?"

My verve came from more than just a feeling of physical fitness. I had evolved through the daily practice of meditation a deeper, inner awareness. By subduing the negative forces that can sink one into the depths of despair, I was able to eliminate the obstacles that had been preventing the free flow of thought and action. My whole spiritual adventure unfolded before me as I became conscious of the power of my mind. Perhaps the greatest test came during a period when someone very close to me suddenly died. My life was torn apart, my roots cruelly pulled up, and I felt bewildered and alone. I lost my will to live. But as time moved on, with each new day I tried desperately to gather inner strength and exert my mental energies to lift myself out of this morass of depression. The wound began to heal slowly and I was able to look ahead and not back to a life that once was. I could then convert the timeless hours that I spent wallowing in sorrow and dejection into positive actions and thoughts that have since opened my life to new adventures.

My enthusiasm for the benefits of yoga turned me into a teacher, lecturer, and writer on the subject. I learned a lot about people from age three to ninety. To my astonishment I discovered that *not all* children are limber. Some are loose-muscled, others tight-muscled, but youth is on their side. In a matter of weeks the tight-muscled children I worked with responded well to the stretching and limbering exercises. It is to be hoped that their early awareness of the body's need for exercise will stay with them through their growing years and into maturity.

My rewards came a thousandfold when I taught arthritics, trapped within their ailing bodies, how to release muscle tension and high-strung executives how to pause for reflection and draw a quiet breath.

By learning to control mind and body, we can get a great deal more out of life. What pleasures can lie ahead when we are able to cope better with tension and learn, in the words of an old Chinese saying, to "bend like the bamboo that does not break as it sways in rhythm with the raging storm." We can learn to survive better under pressure if we know where nature has placed our escape hatches and participate in any competitive sport with greater pleasure and grace. How easy it all becomes once we find the way to let go.

One general word of caution: If you are out of condition, take it easy. Don't rush through this book with a surge of enthusiasm, then drop it a few days later when the results are not immediate. It takes time to restore weak and tense muscles. As you build up your stamina and muscle tone, you will begin to feel a change in your body. Only then will the muscles respond to an increased range of motion, strength, and resilience.

The deep-breathing, relaxation, and mind-control techniques should be followed in the order they are given to achieve the best results. They are designed to help check the frenzy of our lives in a way that even the best exercise and diet programs cannot possibly do.

13

Part I

Chapter 1

Relax, Before You Break Down

The mind and the body are more than married, for they are more
intimately united; and when one suffers, the other sympathizes.
—LORD CHESTERFIELD

"Can you teach me to relax?" a dignified, sixty-year-old pub-
lisher of a national magazine asked me at a dinner party. "I find I
am taking too many tranquilizers and sleeping pills," he added
with embarrassment.

"Learning to relax will take a little time," I told him, "because it
is a gradual mental process."

"How long?" he asked.

"That depends on the person. If you are willing to spend some
time with deep-breathing and mind-control exercises *daily*, it
should take about a week."

"When can we start? Tomorrow?"

The following day my publisher-student arrived promptly,
eager to begin his first lesson in yoga. His composure was decep-
tive. Beneath the camouflage of serenity was a tense, anxious
man, completely wrapped up in his work.

I showed him how to breathe with his diaphragm. The sudden
rush of oxygen to his brain when he took a few deep breaths made
him light-headed. He was a shallow breather and his lungs never
got much exercise; besides, he smoked heavily. I explained to

17

him that a good way to learn to breathe deeply and freely using his diaphragm was for him to lie flat on his back with knees bent. He should place one hand on his abdomen to feel it expanding when he inhaled, then contracting when he exhaled. I told him to think of his breath as a musical cadence that rises and falls with no jerky movements. One can more easily discard the cares of the world and simply let go when the mind is in control.

The muscles around his neck and shoulders were tight. I showed him some tension-release exercises. Rolling his head in a loose, wide circle several times, then rotating his shoulders in a forward and backward motion, seemed to give him quick relief.

Two days later I saw him again. He was jubilant. "I mastered the breathing!" he announced. "It's amazing how that exercise has put me to sleep without a pill!"

With each new yoga session my publisher-student learned different deep-breathing patterns and relaxation techniques. The changes in him became obvious. He was much more relaxed and at ease with himself. He found that he could no longer enjoy smoking. The nicotine irritated his lungs and made him cough. He gave it up without much effort. Some weeks later I received a basket of flowers from him with this note: "The alternate breathing and palming technique saw me through a killer of a day. Took no tranquilizers. Feel great. The word has got around this office that I'm a yoga addict!"

No one can go through life without experiencing tension. It is an essential part of daily living. Even children must learn to cope with their share of anxiety and stress at an early age. The time to be concerned is when tension begins to plague us with symptoms that range from lack of sleep, poor appetite, and loss of weight or the reverse—compulsive eating and weight gain—as well as severe headaches and muscular aches. Other warning signals are when minor problems and disappointments begin to throw us into a state of depression and cause us to suffer the tortures of self-doubt and feelings of inadequacy.

When our emotions pour out distress signals, they leap into action: blood pressure increases, adrenaline flows into the bloodstream, muscles become tense. The results? Migraine and crippling back aches, both of which are frequently traced to the culprit

—tension. And so are many peptic ulcers. Normally, gastric juices enter into a chemical reaction with our food and thus make it digestible. Under stress, the body may secrete many times the usual amount of gastric juices, and their acid can create a hole in the lining of the intestines. When stress disappears, so does the ulcer.

"The coronary-prone individual," says the American Heart Association, "often demonstrates an excessive drive, a sense of time urgency and an immoderate emotional attitude or reaction to stress. Instead of calmly solving his problems by discussing them with someone or trying a new approach, he overreacts to these problems, becoming mentally and physically incapable of resolving them. He is like a machine running with its brakes on with the pressure unable to escape from the engine."

The Middle-Age Blues

There comes a time in our maturing years when each of us experiences the shock that our youth is lost. It strikes us all with varying degrees of intensity. Gray hairs, loss of hair, an expanded waistline, drooping muscles, and decline in physical energy assure us of the grim realization that we have entered middle age. Those in good physical and mental health are more fortunate than others; they survive the middle-age blues with greater fortitude.

Edith, a talented artist friend of mine, was going through the menopausal stage. The estrogen deficiency caused her moods to swing into the depths of depression and anxiety, which brought about regression in her life. She was fifty-one.

"I feel so suicidal," she confided tearfully to me. "John and I are having difficulties in our marriage. He says he can't put up with my depression. Our marriage is finished," she sobbed.

"It doesn't have to be that way," I said, trying to comfort her. "You *can* learn to be calm and in a happier frame of mind through daily meditation."

Edith depended heavily on drugs to maintain her emotional stability. When the drugs wore off, she plunged into despair. Her restless temperament made it extremely difficult for her to sit still.

Her mind was filled with thoughts that never seemed to subside. She was deeply troubled and lost all self-control.

"Try to feel the stillness within yourself," I suggested. "You can achieve this by simply sitting still and allowing your mind to relax. Think of serene and happy thoughts. Every time a negative thought appears, just ignore it and replace it with a pleasant memory. You will gradually train your mind to banish depression, and a sense of calm will take its place."

Edith struggled valiantly to gain self-control. There were times, however, when she was so obsessed by depression that she didn't care whether she lived or not. During one of our yoga sessions I showed her the candle concentration exercise designed to harness the mind by directing it solely to the orange flame that burned brightly. She found this mind training exercise helpful. Each day she sat for about ten minutes and gazed at the candle flame. Her power of concentration increased greatly. When she closed her eyes, she could retain the image of the flame for a few minutes and think of nothing else. Her ability to sit still made it possible for her to enjoy quiet moments of deep reflection. It took about three months before she gained sufficient mental stability so that she no longer had to depend on drugs. She found herself back in her studio painting. Her creative energies began to soar. She painted with sensitivity and expression. At a recent exhibition of her works her husband escorted me through the gallery. "Isn't Edith terrific?" he asked, smiling proudly.

The Importance of Exercise

"The average American settles down at about twenty-five to a life of physical inactivity," says the American Heart Association. "When he does get exercise he tends to overdo it—and strains his out-of-shape body. It's never too late to begin to improve your physical condition. But a thorough physical exam is an essential first step in order to learn what you can safely do."

Whether you spend a great part of your working life at your office or home, the chances are that you do not find the time in the mornings to exercise. By evening you are too tired to move a muscle. You look forward to a relaxing hour before dinner with a cocktail or two. If you have a good appetite, you eat well.

Take a close look at yourself in the mirror. Are you in shape? If not, what happened to that once taut figure you had in your active youth? By not exercising to burn up excess calories your muscles have become flabby and tense; your energy lags. What about your posture? Perhaps the shoulders have slumped a little, the thighs have spread, the underarms are a bit flabby, and there is possibly some extra padding around the middle. Does this picture describe you in any way? If so, don't shrug it off with a laugh and attribute these changes to getting on in years. Flabbiness and overweight are unnecessary partners in our maturing life.

Habit is hard to break. Once you have become accustomed to a behavioral pattern—whatever it may be—you tend to adhere to it. Exercise is an example. If you are unaccustomed to a daily routine of maintaining your level of physical fitness, you will readily find a number of excuses to justify reasons for not exercising. But you *can* make habit work for you, not against you.

The effort to establish a standard of physical fitness will pay off when you consider the benefits gained. By exercising daily, your muscles will become longer and more flexible. All your joints will begin to feel loose and free. As the circulation steps up through deep breathing exercises, your general condition will improve considerably.

Exercises play a great part in the therapy for arthritis, since most joint weakness and disability in common arthritis come from poor muscular tone in those muscles close to the affected joint. Exercise builds up internal heat and increases circulation, thus providing relief from pain.

The late, eminent heart specialist Dr. Paul Dudley White endorsed regular exercise and physical activity as part of a general prescription to protect the heart and help prevent premature heart attacks and strokes. He advocated bicycling, walking, and other leg-power activity as often as possible. Dr. White followed his own advice. In the early hours of the morning this vigorous man in his seventies bicycled daily, pedaling the wheels with tremendous verve. Dr. White firmly believed that hard work never hurt a healthy human being.

With its built-in ability of self-repair the body can work miraculously if it is properly nourished and given adequate exercise and rest. We can live to a ripe old age without the parts breaking down. "Most aging is premature," according to Dr. Thomas Gardiner, one of the founders of the National Foundation for Anti-Aging Research. He stated that we haven't even approached what could be the normal span of years. Body organs seem designed to last six or seven times as long as it usually takes the average person to reach maturity. This does not mean that we would have to add useless years to old age; it means staying young longer. Known for his work with vitamins, Dr. Gardiner said that "if we apply what we know about nutrition, we could double our life span."

His theory of longevity holds true for the Hunzakuts. A high percentage of them live to be more than 100 and look half their years. Some 40,000 Hunzakuts live in the land of Hunza. This is in the Karakoram Range of Pakistani-controlled Kashmir in northern India. These people inspired James Hilton to write *Lost Horizon.*

The late Dr. Robert McCarrison spent many years living among the Hunzakuts to observe their way of life. He concluded that their excellent health is attributed to three simple factors: healthy diet, vigorous physical exercise, and adequate rest.

There are two other groups alleged to live unusually long lives. The Ecuadorans in the Andean village of Vilcabamba and the Abkhazia in the Georgian Soviet Union. The people of these three cultures all do hard physical work, live in relatively remote mountainous areas, and have robust health and remarkable longevity.

With the scientific knowledge that is ours today, it should be possible for us to follow an intelligent course in prolonging our lives. Yet by the time we reach the age of sixty-five to seventy, our bodies are worn out. We may be knowledgeable about the nature and workings of the machines we invent, but we are often ignorant and uncaring about the workings of our own bodies. Would we ever dare abuse our automobiles or any other machine as we do ourselves? We know that such abuse of the machine would undoubtedly cause expensive breakdowns. Don't our bodies deserve better treatment?

Our life-style is frenetic, our diet mostly unbalanced. We rush day after day, hour after hour, tense and exhausted. The important thing is to get ahead at any price. Have you ever watched a crowd at a rush hour? Seldom will you find one person walking less hurriedly than the rest. Everyone seems tense and trying to push ahead of the person in front. What about drivers in their automobiles? They sit tensely gripping the steering wheel, tempers ready to flare, all set to shout or blow the horn if another car happens to get ahead. Why all the hurry? We are all guilty of this kind of false urgency in racing to catch a particular train or plane at any cost or pushing ourselves beyond physical endurance because *we must get ahead.* When this kind of tension builds up, the body breaks down and the heart simply gives up.

When we are advised by our doctors or friends to slow down, we should do just that—*slow down and enjoy life while we can.* Why rush through life as if we were facing an ultimate crisis every day? Learn to relax. It will pay off.

Dr. George S. Stevenson, former president of the American Psychiatric Association and of the World Federation of Mental Health, advocates some simple ways to ease the pressures of everyday living. These are excerpts from his booklet, *How to Deal With Your Tensions,* issued by the National Association for Mental Health:

1. TALK IT OUT. When something worries you, talk it out. Don't bottle it up. Confide your worry to some levelheaded person you can trust; your husband or wife, father or mother, a good friend, your clergyman, your family doctor, a teacher, school counselor, or dean. Talking things out helps to relieve your strain, helps you to see your worry in a clearer light, and often helps you to see what you can do about it.

2. ESCAPE FOR AWHILE. Sometimes, when things go wrong, it helps to escape from the painful problem *for a while:*

to lose yourself in a movie, or a book or a game, or a brief trip for a change of scene. Making yourself "stand there and suffer" is a form of self-punishment, not a way to solve a problem. It is perfectly realistic and healthy to escape punishment long enough to recover breath and balance. But be prepared to come back and deal with your difficulty when you are more composed, and when you and others involved are in better condition to deal with it.

3. WORK OFF YOUR ANGER. If you feel yourself using anger as a general way of behavior, remember that while anger may give you a temporary sense of righteousness, or even of power, it will generally leave you feeling foolish and sorry in the end. If you feel like lashing out at someone who has provoked you, try holding off that impulse for awhile. Let it wait until tomorrow. Meanwhile, do something constructive with the pent-up energy. Pitch into some physical activity like gardening, cleaning out the garage, carpentry or some other do-it-yourself project. Or work it out in tennis or a long walk. Working the anger out of your system and cooling it off for a day or two will leave you much better prepared to handle your problem.

4. GIVE IN OCCASIONALLY. If you find yourself getting into frequent quarrels with people, and feeling obstinate and defiant, remember that that's the way frustrated children behave. Stand your ground on what you know is right, but do so calmly and make allowance for the fact that you *could* turn out to be wrong. And even if you're dead right, it's easier on your system to give in once in awhile. If you yield, you'll usually find the others will, too. And if you can work this out, the result will be relief from tension, the achievement of a practical solution, together with a great feeling of satisfaction and maturity.

5. DO SOMETHING FOR OTHERS. If you feel yourself worrying about *yourself* all the time, try *doing* something for *somebody else*. You'll find this will take the steam out of your own worries and—even better—give you a fine feeling of having done well.

6. TAKE ONE THING AT A TIME. For people under tension, an ordinary work load can sometimes seem unbearable. The load looks so great that it becomes painful to tackle any part of it—even the things that most need to be done. When that happens, remember that it's a temporary condition and that you can work your way out of it. The surest way to do this is to take a few of the most urgent tasks and pitch into them, one at a time, setting aside all the rest for the time being. Once you dispose of these you'll see that the remainder is not such a "horrible mess" after all. You'll be in the swing of things, and the rest of the tasks will go much more easily. If you feel you can't set anything aside to tackle things this sensible way, reflect: are you sure you aren't overestimating the importance of the things you do—that is, your own importance?

7. SHUN THE "SUPERMAN" URGE. Some people expect too much from themselves, and get into a constant state of worry and anxiety because they think they are not achieving as much as they should. They try for perfection in everything. Admirable as this ideal is, it is an open invitation to failure. No one can be perfect in everything. Decide which things you do well, and then put your major effort into these. They are apt to be the things you like to do and, hence, those that give you most satisfaction. Then, perhaps, come the things you can't do so well. Give them the best of your effort and ability, but don't take yourself to task if you can't achieve the impossible.

8. GO EASY WITH YOUR CRITICISM. Some people expect too much of others, and then feel frustrated, let down, disappointed, even "trapped" when another person does not measure up. The "other person" may be a wife, a husband or a child whom we are trying to fit into a preconceived pattern —perhaps even trying to make over to suit ourselves. Remember, each person has his own virtues, his own shortcomings, his own values, his own right to develop as an individual. People who feel let down by the shortcomings (real or imagined) of their relatives, are really let down about themselves.

Instead of being critical about the other person's behavior, search out the good points and help him to develop them. This will give both of you satisfaction and help you to gain a better perspective on yourself as well.

9. GIVE THE OTHER FELLOW A BREAK. When people are under emotional tension, they often feel that they have to "get there first"—to edge out the other person, no matter if the goal is as trivial as getting ahead on the highway. If enough of us feel that way—and many of us do—then everything becomes a race in which somebody is bound to get injured—physically, as on the highway, or emotionally and mentally, in the endeavor to live a full life. It need not be this way. Competition is contagious, but so is cooperation. When you give the other fellow a break, you very often make things easier for yourself; if he no longer feels you are a threat to him, he stops being a threat to you.

10. MAKE YOURSELF "AVAILABLE." Many of us have the feeling that we are being "left out," slighted, neglected, rejected. Often, we just imagine that other people feel this way about us, when in reality they are eager for us to make the first move. It may be we, not the others, who are depreciating ourselves. Instead of shrinking away and withdrawing, it is much healthier, as well as more practical, to continue to "make yourself available"—to make some of the overtures instead of always waiting to be asked. Of course, the opposite of withdrawal is equally futile; to push yourself forward on every occasion. This is often misinterpreted and may lead to real rejection. There is a middle ground. Try it.

11. SCHEDULE YOUR RECREATION. Many people drive themselves so hard that they allow themselves too little time for recreation—an essential for good physical and mental health. They find it hard to make themselves take time out. For such people a set routine and schedule will help—a program of definite hours when they will engage in some recreation. And in general it is desirable for almost everyone to have a hobby

that absorbs him in off hours—one into which he can throw himself completely and with pleasure, forgetting all about his work.

Chapter 2

Deep Breathing, the Elixir of Life

Mind is the master of the senses, and breath is the master of the mind.

—HATHA YOGA PRADIPIKA

There is a delightful Indian parable that describes a dispute among the powers of the body, each claiming to be the one indispensable force. The powers finally agreed that to prove their worth, each would take leave of the body individually to judge how the others would survive by themselves.

The eyes were the first to depart. On returning after a year's absence, they asked: "How have you lived without us?"

And the powers replied: "Like blind people we have lived. Not seeing with the eyes, but breathing with the breath, speaking with the tongue, hearing with the ears, knowing with the mind, and generating with the seed. Thus have we lived."

When the ears departed and returned, the powers gave this answer: "Like deaf people we have lived, but with the help of all the others we have been able to exist."

Then the tongue took leave, and it was given a similar answer on its return: "Like dumb people we have lived," said the powers, "but we have managed by pulling our forces together."

Next the mind took leave of the body. For a year the powers struggled. "We have lived like fools without you," they told the

29

mind when it returned, "but we were able to exist, for we all stood united."

The departure of the seed caused the body and mind great anguish. They told the seed on its return: "Without you we have been barren, but we have managed to exist."

Now it was time for the breath to take leave of the body. But the breath warned the other powers, saying: "Gentlemen, don't deceive yourselves. It is I alone dividing myself fivefold who keep together this body and support it."

But the powers insisted that the breath be tested. Just as the breath rose and appeared to be leaving, the body was torn apart.

"Sir," the powers cried, "don't leave us! You are indeed the supreme ruler of us all."

The yogis discovered centuries ago that breathing is the elixir of life. They developed it into an empirical science and art that could be applied in different rhythmic patterns to every human need. There is a way to step up mental performance through a brisk supply of oxygen to the brain cells. By flushing the bloodstream with oxygen, the cells in the body are revitalized. A reservoir of energy can be slowly gathered, focused, and then directed through the body to strengthen the lungs and develop a strong, efficient heart. This builds up recuperative powers, calms the nerves, induces restful sleep, and slows down the aging process.

These breathing patterns have a bracing effect and build resistance to colds and other respiratory ailments. Asthmatics can benefit from the long drawn-out breathing vibrations to increase the stamina of their lungs and reduce muscle tension. Smokers who suffer from shortness of breath can apply deep-breathing techniques to clear their lungs of congestion. Some even lose their desire to smoke.

By pumping oxygen to the brain through deep-breathing exercises, we can wake up the brain cells. This can be particularly helpful to senile or elderly persons. An interesting experiment was made on such people in 1969 by clinical psychologists at the Veterans Administration Hospital in Buffalo, New York.[*]

---

[*] Eleanor A. Jacobs, Ph.D., Peter W. Winter, M.D., Harry J. Alvis, M.D., and S. Mouchly Small, M.D., "Hyperbaric Oxygen Effect on Cognition and Behavior in the Aged," reprinted from Jules H. Masserman, M.D., ed., *Current Psychiatric Therapies*, Vol. II. New York, Grune & Stratton, 1971.

Thirteen elderly men were placed in a pressurized chamber and exposed intermittently to 100 percent oxygen. After two treatments daily for fifteen days the patients showed as much as a 25 percent increase on the standard memory tests. The oxygen treatment had stimulated their brain cells and increased their vitality.

Most of us are unaware of the untapped resources of body and mind. When the simple matter of breathing is brought to our attention, we are surprised to learn that we use only a third of our lung capacity. Most of us coast on shallow breathing. Normally, we breathe about sixteen times a minute and take in a pint of air each time. This only partially inflates the lungs, which can hold eight times as much air.

Learning to breathe with the diaphragm will overcome shallow, lazy breathing by getting more air into the lungs. Vigorous breathing massages the liver and spleen and helps the circulation of blood back to the heart so the blood can return to the lungs for pure oxygen.

Your diaphragm is the principal muscle used in breathing. It is dome-shaped and forms the floor of the chest. When you take a proper deep, full breath, the lower, middle, and upper portions of the lungs get a full supply of oxygen. As we breathe in, expanding the abdomen, air enters the lower lobes. (See diagram.) The diaphragm descends. Air is drawn up to the middle and upper portions of the lungs, which causes the ribcage to move out and the chest to expand. The process is reversed when we exhale: The diaphragm rises as air leaves the upper and middle portions of the lungs, allowing the chest and rib cage to close in. Finally, when the air leaves the lower lobes, the abdomen is drawn in.

This process of respiration is done in a continuous, flowing rhythm, as if pouring water into a pitcher: first the bottom, then the middle, and finally the top. When emptying, the top is first, then the middle, and lastly the bottom.

The lungs act as a bellows when air is pumped vigorously in and out of them. This increases their tone and resilience. Unfortunately most of us are taught in early youth the reverse of correct breathing: "Chest out! Belly in!" was the usual reprimand of the gym instructor. No animal or infant breathes this way. The natural instinct is the direct opposite.

Most yogic breathing patterns, with few exceptions, emphasize the importance of inhaling and exhaling through the nostrils. The reason is that the air-cleaning process for the lungs begins with hairs in the nose that act as a vacuum cleaner, trapping dust particles that enter the nose. When we breathe out through the nostrils rather than through the mouth, the lungs gain more stamina, since they take a longer time to deflate. Test this reaction by lifting something requiring physical energy, such as a heavy chair. You will find that your stamina is increased if you inhale deeply

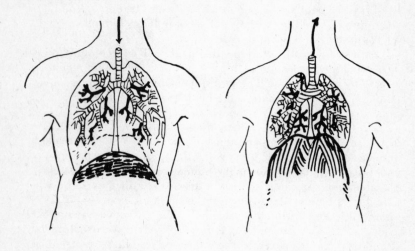

ACTION OF THE DIAPHRAGM. When we breathe in, the diaphragm expands downward and the ribs move out so that the chest cavity increases and the lungs fill with air. When we breathe out, the diaphragm rises and the ribs close in, reducing the chest cavity. The lungs become compressed when they expel air.

through your nostrils, hold your breath as long as possible, then slowly release the air through your nostrils. The power of your breath is strengthened and prolonged while you concentrate on the slow expulsion of air from your lungs.

If your lungs are not strong and you quickly run out of breath or have difficulty blowing out a candle flame or inflating a paper bag or balloon, the deep-breathing exercises given in this chapter will help strengthen weak lungs.

The first step is to learn to breathe with your diaphragm—the way infants and opera singers do; it is also the way we breathe when asleep. Once you get the knack of it, you will breathe this way unconsciously.

All the breathing exercises should be practiced in the order they are given to gradually strengthen the lungs and develop ease with the different rhythmic patterns.

Deep-Breathing Exercises

DIAPHRAGMATIC BREATHING
(to calm your nerves and induce restful sleep)

The purpose of Diaphragmatic Breathing is to stretch the lower lobes of the lungs with more air. This low, quiet breathing will calm emotions and induce restful sleep. It can be done either lying flat or sitting in a chair. Be sure to loosen your belt and collar. If you are sitting, place your hands limply on the thighs; spine straight but not rigid. If you are lying on your back, bend your knees with feet drawn to the buttocks and arms to your sides. It will help to place one hand on your abdomen and the other on your chest. The emphasis of breathing is on the abdomen. The chest is relaxed.

Inhale deeply through the nostrils and *expand* the abdomen. Keep your shoulders and chest relaxed.

Exhale slowly through the nostrils while *pulling in the abdomen to the back of the spine.*

When you are able to control your breathing in this way, concentrate on maintaining a steady rhythmic pattern:

Inhale to the count of 5 seconds.
Exhale to the count of 10 seconds.

Repeat this pattern 10 to 15 times a day. You will begin to feel the ease and flow of your breath taking control of the body. Be as relaxed as you can. Keep your eyes closed.

33

COMPLETE BREATH
(to recharge your energy)

This breathing pattern is the second step to the basic Diaphragmatic Breathing. You start with a partial abdominal breath, then continue to inhale, bringing the air up to the rib cage, then to the topmost part of the lungs, expanding the chest. It is done with one continuous breath.

Since this breathing technique is deep and brings a rush of oxygen to the brain, you may feel a little light-headed at first if you are unaccustomed to deep breathing. This is caused by hyperventilation, which will disappear with continued practice of deep breathing.

You can do this exercise lying on your back, sitting, or standing. It is an exhilarating way to wake up the brain cells in the morning or pick up your energy as it lags during the course of the day.

Your breath is drawn in one continuous motion. Inhale slowly through the nostrils, expanding the abdomen. When the air enters the lower lobes of the lungs, continue to inhale, pulling the air up as the rib cage moves out to increase the chest cavity. Draw the air all the way up to fully inflate your lungs. Try not to be tense. Let your shoulders rise freely. Now exhale slowly through the nostrils, drawing in your abdomen. Allow the air to be released very quietly and smoothly while your rib cage closes in, reducing your chest cavity. When the lungs become compressed, the air is completely expelled.

Repeat the same breathing pattern with your eyes closed, following this ratio:

> Inhale to the count of 5 seconds.
> Hold your breath for 20 seconds.
> Exhale to the count of 10 seconds.

Repeat the same exercise. This time stretch your arms over your head as you inhale deeply, fully inflating your lungs. Hold your breath and feel the energy surging through your body. Then, as you exhale, drop your arms limply to your sides, expelling all air as you release tension.

Repeat 5 times without stopping whenever you want to re-charge your energy.

ALTERNATE BREATHING
(excellent for tension headaches)

Once you have learned to breathe easily with your diaphragm, the Alternate Breathing exercise will be most helpful in relieving tension headaches and opening up the sinus passages. If your nostrils are blocked, simply press your right thumb on your right nostril. Then forcibly inhale and exhale through the left nostril, 10 to 15 times. Repeat the same forceful breathing through the right nostril.

For the Alternate Breathing, sit comfortably in a chair with your legs slightly apart and feet flat on the floor. Keep your spine straight, but not rigid.

Place the right thumb on the right nostril (index and middle fingers turned in). The fourth and little fingers are placed near the left nostril.

With the thumb pressing the right nostril, inhale deeply (expanding the abdomen) to the count of 5 seconds through the left nostril.

Close the left nostril with the fourth finger. Release the right nostril and exhale (pulling in the abdomen) to the count of 10 seconds.

Without stopping, inhale again through the *right* nostril to the count of 5 seconds.

Close that nostril with the thumb. Release the left nostril and exhale completely to the count of 10 seconds.

This is the key to one round of Alternate Breathing. It should be done in a continuous flow without staggering the breath. Think of your breath as a thin silken thread that rises and falls with a musical cadence. The thread will snap if you stagger your breath.

As you become more proficient in this pattern of deep breathing, you will feel a sense of deep calm when the tension dissolves.

Gradually increase the ratio of your breathing pattern as your lungs gain more stamina. Repeat each round three times without stopping.

ONE ROUND

INHALE to the count of .... 6 seconds
EXHALE .... 12 seconds
INHALE .... 6 seconds
EXHALE .... 12 seconds

INHALE to the count of .... 7 seconds
EXHALE .... 14 seconds
INHALE .... 7 seconds
EXHALE .... 14 seconds

INHALE to the count of .... 8 seconds
EXHALE .... 16 seconds
INHALE .... 8 seconds
EXHALE .... 16 seconds

SIGHING BREATH
(to release overworked emotions)

This effective breathing technique will rapidly quiet the mind. It is a good escape hatch for pent-up tension and can be done anywhere: standing while waiting for a bus or elevator or during anxious moments when time begins to drag. Rather than pace up and down, calm yourself with the Sighing Breath.

Inhale deeply through the nostrils, filling your lungs with air. Then exhale slowly through your mouth with lips puckered, as if cooling soup. The sound should be a long, heaving sigh. If you concentrate on this release of emotions, you will begin to feel the tension knots dissolving.

The deeper your concentration, the calmer you will become. Prolong the exhalation as much as possible.

To feel the effect of this exercise, it should be repeated at least 10 times continuously. By breathing this way, rather than short, quick breaths, the normal carbon dioxide-oxygen content of the blood will be restored. The more air that is let out of the lungs during expiration, the more tension release occurs. It takes muscular control to exhale twice the ratio that you inhale; therefore, it is important to relax mentally and be consciously aware of loosening the deeply embedded tension.

HEALING BREATH
(to release tension caused by physical pain)

The Healing Breath can have a powerful effect on the mind to a point where pain can actually be banished if it is practiced with sufficient concentration.

Concentrate on the area of the pain. Then inhale deeply and visualize that you are absorbing all the forces of healing energy through the pores of your skin. Gather this energy and focus its strength on the area of the pain. Feel the warm blood coursing through your body—through your arms, through your legs, and through your torso. Don't tense up.

As you exhale deeply, feel your shoulders beginning to sink, your head dropping, and your arms and legs becoming heavy and limp. Keep your mind within your body. Continue to feel the warm blood flow. The pain will slowly decrease as you enter into a deeper state of relaxation. Continue to breathe deeply, letting yourself sink further and further into deeper levels of serenity.

UPPER RESPIRATORY TRACT

1. FRONTAL SINUS
2. NASAL CAVITY
3. BASE OF TONGUE
4. PHARYNX
5. LARYNX OR VOICE BOX
6. TRACHEA

LISTEN TO THE SOUND OF YOUR BREATH
(to increase blood flow and energy)

This breathing exercise will help you tune in to the more subtle sounds of your body to develop inner awareness of blood flow and energy. It will leave you calm and revitalized.

Inhale deeply and quietly through your nostrils to create a sound similar to a gentle snore. Feel the coolness of the air

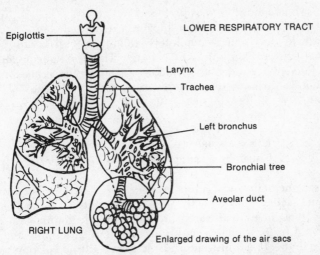

LOWER RESPIRATORY TRACT

Epiglottis

Larynx

Trachea

Left bronchus

Bronchial tree

Aveolar duct

RIGHT LUNG

Enlarged drawing of the air sacs

The alveoli (air sacs) enveloped as they are by networks of capillaries, provide spaces where gases can diffuse between air and blood. The air exchange takes place in the alveoli.

passing up through the frontal sinus behind the bridge of your nose. (See diagrams.) Be aware of its energy as your breath travels upward into your head, waking up your brain cells.

Follow it as it travels down the larynx, or voice box, as you exhale in the same gentle snore. Feel its energy in your throat. Listen to its vibrations as it moves steadily downward. Inhale deeply again. Hold your breath and contract the abdominal muscles, drawing them up under the diaphragm and back toward the spine. This creates what the yogis call a "solar-plexus lock" (network of nerves at upper part of the abdomen) and automatically locks the sphincter muscles in the rectum. By contracting these muscles, at the same time holding your breath, an internal pressure is created that produces a stimulating effect on the nerve centers located in these areas, vitalizing the entire nervous system.

Feel the energy expanding in your body and spreading into your groin and other vital areas. Hold your breath as long as possible without straining to stimulate the exchange of gases.

The oxygen nourishes your bloodstream, tissues, and lungs, while the waste gas, carbon dioxide, is expelled.

Exhale slowly and completely, following your breath as it travels upward and out of your lungs. Think of your breath as the force of life and energy, and use its power to the maximum.

Repeat this excellent energy pickup several times a day, whenever you feel the need.

RUNNER'S BREATH
(excellent antidepressant; restores vitality)

This is one of the most exhilarating exercises in deep breathing. Its quick action increases the blood's capacity to absorb more oxygen than in normal, deep breathing. While toning the diaphragm, it restores vitality and is an excellent antidepressant.

Though this breathing pattern is done in a sitting position with the body still, it is called the Runner's Breath because the lungs, diaphragm, and abdominal muscles are exerted to their utmost as in running. It is also known as the Bellows Breath, for the lungs act as a bellows in the quick expulsion of air. This is not an easy exercise. It does take practice to acquire the right, brisk rhythm. Emphasis is on the *forceful expulsion* of carbon dioxide through the nostrils, similar to outward sniffs creating a staccato rhythm. Inhalation of fresh oxygen becomes an *involuntary movement*—a reaction to the conscious act of expulsion, as in a bellows. Its sound is not heard after the staccato rhythm of exhalation.

Sit comfortably in a chair with spine straight, feet flat on the floor, and hands resting on the thighs. Eyes closed.

Exhale forcefully through the nose; *at the same time* contract the abdomen to expel air. There should be a powerful push from the diaphragm and thrust from the throat. *Without stopping,* release the contraction, and the lungs will automatically take in fresh oxygen. *Try not to inhale. This is done properly only as an involuntary action.*

The stages of learning the Runner's Breath are slow, so be patient if you want to achieve it. At first practice this exercise slowly to maintain an even staccato rhythm. It should sound like the tick of a clock, sending out the signals of the seconds . . . 1 and 2, and 3 and 4, maintaining an even rhythm. Then gradually build up to 10 expulsions. The tempo should be: 1 and 2, and 3 and 4, and 5 and 6, and 7 and 8, and 9 and 10. Stop, inhale deeply to fill the lungs with air. Exhale and relax.

Repeat 5 times from 1 to 10 without stopping.

Remember that the emphasis is on exhalation.

When you are able to do 10 expulsions with an even, sharp rhythm, slowly build up the expulsions to 20, 30, 40, 50, and up to 100. Once you have developed the technique, you can easily go on beyond that.

I showed the Runner's Breath to a young college student who practiced it until he was able to apply its power to his middle-distance running. Some months later, when I saw him again, he was exuberant.

"You have no idea what you have done for me!" he exclaimed. "I can run at a much faster pace and for a longer time without feeling the painful bursting of my lungs . . . and you should have seen me at the handball court. That was something! I exhausted my opponent because I can now quickly recharge my energy with this breathing technique. It's terrific!"

His enthusiasm was contagious.

"Do you realize," I said to him, "that if more young athletes learned the Runner's Breath, it might revolutionize the basic training in track? I run in place one thousand times every morning using the Runner's Breath. My lungs are never exhausted because I am constantly pumping out the carbon dioxide as a continuous fresh supply of oxygen is inhaled automatically."

"Want to meet my coach?" he asked.

"I certainly do!"

Chapter 3

Harmony of Body and Mind

Control over thought is a long, painful and laborious process. But I am convinced that no time, no labor, and no pain is too much for the glorious result to be reached.

—GANDHI

Activity and rest make up the rhythm of life. We can see it in the harmony of nature itself. Time to grow and time to rest. But our frenetic life-style does not permit this harmonious balance. We are propelled, at a speed measured by formulas, with one eye on the clock and the other on a rushed existence. Few of us have the capacity to relax and dismiss all the cares and worry in moments of needed rest. This is surely one of the secrets shared by all great men and women. They know the importance of relaxation. The rhythm of life swings between involvement and withdrawal, action and thought.

Unlike Westerners, Orientals are taught to tune in to the soft signals of the body and mind. To listen to its internal rhythm, to feel the blood flow, to hear the heart beat, to sit in a quiet place and meditate seem contrary to our puritanical compulsion to always be "doing something useful"—or at least appear so.

Some years ago when I was traveling in New Delhi, I met a frail sadhu, a religious holy man. It was a hot, sultry day. He was ambling slowly on the dusty road, deep in contemplation, with a wooden bowl under his arm. His garment was threadbare and his hair disheveled.

I asked my Indian driver to stop the car and offer the sadhu a lift. The driver was dismayed and thought this a strange gesture.

"If madam wishes, I will stop," he said.

The sadhu bowed with his palms together in a gesture of saluta-tion when I offered him a ride.

"It is not necessary," he said softly. "I am not in a hurry."

"Then can we give you something to drink?" I asked.

"I will accept with pleasure."

We stopped at a street stall nearby and he drank some orange juice. He asked me questions about myself and what I was doing in India. I told him I was traveling for pleasure and partly to do some research on a book I was writing. When he learned that I was deeply interested in yoga, he waxed lyrical with philosophi-ical sayings:

"You do not have to come to India to find inner peace. You must find it in yourself," he said, waving his right index finger in the air with the gesture of authority.

"If you wish to be inwardly calm, think of your mind as a lake and your actions quivering over the surface of this lake. Now if the surface is smooth, without even a ripple, then you will be able to see the image of your true self reflected on its unbroken surface. . . . You should meditate on this," he added.

He reflected awhile, then his dark, penetrating eyes looked at me.

"To be in tune with this world we must first be in tune with ourselves; only then can we move on to higher levels of con-sciousness."

With these words of wisdom he placed the palms of his hands together, head bowed, and bade me farewell.

*"Om, shanti, shanti, shanti,"** he chanted as he walked on with the wooden bowl under his arm.

"He begs for food," my driver explained. "He owns nothing except . . . maybe his own happiness."

The life of a sadhu is a chosen one, and only a select few wish it. But we have something to learn from this solitary soul who walks the earth alone. He has indeed found his inner peace.

**Om* is a Sanskrit word; it is also spelled *aum.* It signifies A: evolution, U: preservation, M: dissolution. Life begins and ends with *om. Shanti* means peace.

To most of us whose lives are fraught with frustrations and challenge, relaxation does not come easily. At first it must be a controlled process to unite body and mind so they can respond to each other and become attuned and balanced in themselves. When we ignore the need for physical and mental relaxation, our nerves, muscles, and emotions become overstrained through excessive activity not broken by repose. Continued nerve-muscle tension will break down the body's rhythmic control. Sometimes our tensions may be so deep that we are unaware of them. It is the control of tension that we must master. This is the key to relaxation. Deep relaxation gives the body and mind a chance to recuperate. Reading, watching a play or movie, participating in sports are all more superficial forms of relaxation. The mind does not rest, and the inner tensions of the body persist. Even during sleep the mind and body frequently do not rest. The mind continues to be active in low-level worries, in planning, and in dreaming. Deep relaxation will not occur unless the mind participates, and only meditation rests the mind completely.

Knowing how to relax will help break our emotional behavioral pattern in the way we instinctively react to constant stress and tension. Anger, worry, and fear play havoc with our nervous system. What happens when we respond to a flood of irritations? A surge of anger blazes within us, evoking muscle tension. The neck and shoulders stiffen. Changes in blood circulation and heart action cause our breathing to become short and erratic. The pulse quickens. When the digestive system is under attack, we feel severe stomach cramps or become nauseated.

Anger makes us lose full possession of our faculties, and frequently we will act irrationally, later regretting our behavior. When we are in a state of frenzy, we lose our focus in seeing things as they really are.

What can we do about it? We can change some of our behavioral patterns to maintain our equilibrium under stress by applying some simple and basic principles of relaxation and mind control. Those given in this chapter will help you learn to relax the muscles, reduce sympathetic nervous activity, control overworked emotions, and quiet rambling thoughts. You can learn to slow down and give yourself a chance to recuperate from long periods of strenuous work. Most of us work too hard and are frequently unaware of our built-up tension and irritability until we collapse from the strain. Since we spend so much time sitting, we should learn to relax in this position.

Let your spinal column carry the weight of your body as nature intended. Balance yourself so that the full weight of the body is distributed evenly and is not sagging to one side. Place a small cushion to support your spine in a straight-backed chair. This will give you maximum freedom from muscle strain. Keep your feet on the floor. When your body is perfectly balanced, you can sit this way comfortably for hours while typing, writing, reading, or doing anything that confines you to a chair.

EXPERIENCE TOTAL RELAXATION

Try this when you have at least ten minutes to spare. Remove your shoes to give your feet free circulation. Loosen any clothing that hampers your breathing, particularly around the neck and waist. Keep your hands relaxed. Place them on your lap, or interlock the fingers loosely. Your feet should rest on the floor so your body weight is evenly distributed. Keep your back straight but not rigid. It will be more comfortable to lean slightly against a straight-backed chair.

Be sure that you can start the process of relaxation without any interruption. *This is important.* At first relaxing may take longer than ten minutes before you are able to completely coax your muscles to let go. It becomes easier with daily practice. When physical relaxation is mastered, mental relaxation follows easily and naturally.

Read through the following instructions to memorize the order of letting the muscles go, then close your eyes and proceed.

Keep your breathing deep, slow, and quiet. The entire respiratory cycle should take about 15 seconds: 5 seconds of deep inhalation and 10 seconds of slow exhalation. Breathe in and out of the nostrils.

Gently coax your muscles to relax. Speak to yourself slowly, in simple, self-directed phrases, so the words become effective through repetition. Say to yourself: *I feel quiet. . . . I am calm. . . . My body is relaxed. . . . I feel each muscle becoming limp.*

Start relaxing the muscles of your feet. Feel each toe becoming limp. Then slowly work on the instep and ankle of each foot separately. Again repeating, *I am relaxing each toe. Now it is relaxed. It feels limp.*

By concentrating deeply, you can feel the waves of relaxation creeping into your legs. Slowly stretch your right leg, contracting the muscles. Relax it by pulling the muscles back to normal in the same length of time it took to stretch them. By using a little resistance, a slight stretching occurs in other adjacent muscles that are not ordinarily exercised. Repeat with the left leg.

Then raise the right foot, wiggle the toes and ankles. Repeat with the left foot. This will increase blood circulation. Concentrate on the warm waves of relaxation now spreading into your thighs, hips, abdomen, and chest. Continue to breathe deeply and quietly through your nostrils. Tense your torso, then relax it. Pull your shoulders back, then let them sag. Rotate them slowly in a circle: up, back, down, forward. Repeat 5 times to feel tension knots loosening. Now be aware of the blood coursing through your arms and down through your body. Feel the warmth of your hands extending to each fingertip. Stretch the fingers apart and relax them. Make a tight fist with both hands, then relax them. Wiggle the hands as if shaking drops of water from the fingertips.

Now relax the neck and facial muscles. Roll your head gently in a circle: forward and down, right, back, left. Repeat this rolling motion 5 times, then reverse the movement.

It helps to relax the facial and throat muscles. First relax your jaw so the teeth don't grind. Feel the root of your tongue relaxing. Mentally erase deep stress lines in your face and around your eyes. Then smile to stretch those muscles.

Now imagine that your eyes are sinking gently back into their sockets. Concentrate on loosening the tension in the eyeballs and eyelids. Feel the tension slowly dissolving as you enter into a deeper state of relaxation.

Listen to your heartbeat. Listen to its strong, steady rhythm beating at an even pace. Feel the warm blood coursing through your body. Your nerves are slowly unwinding.

Inhale deeply and be conscious of your breath. Know its power to restore energy into your body and to quiet you when you need rest. Exhale slowly. You are now effortlessly allowing your body to drift more and more into a deeper state of relaxation. You feel a sense of lightness, as if you were floating. You are releasing deeply embedded muscle tension.

Slowly stand up and stretch your arms over your head. Take a deep, full breath, stretch upward, then bend forward, letting your arms drop down without resistance.

Slowly touch your toes or as far down as you can reach. Come up gradually. Take another deep breath. Now you should feel relaxed yet recharged with energy.

WAYS TO INDUCE RESTFUL SLEEP

Don't fight insomnia. If you are a restless sleeper, try these helpful ways to release the burden of worry, anxiety, and tension that rob you of a good night's sleep.

Take a brisk walk after dinner. A little cool night air and exercise will induce sleep. If this is not possible, wait an hour after dinner, then take a warm bath. Relax in the tub while listening to soothing music. You will soon feel the tension knots dissolving. When drying yourself, don't use the towel for brisk rubbing; just remove excess moisture by patting the towel on your skin.

Before going to sleep, drink a glass of warm milk as a mild sedative. Be sure your bedroom is well ventilated. An over-heated bedroom will dry up the mucus in your nostrils and throat and give you a stuffy head.

Turn off all lights except a night-light if you are accustomed to using one. There should be no constriction in your nightclothes to hamper your breathing. If you can sleep in the nude, all the better.

While in bed, lie on your back with arms loosely by your sides and legs bent. Tuck a large, soft pillow under the knees and a thin soft one under the head so your neck will relax more easily.

Now that the setting is conducive to a quiet and restful atmosphere, begin to coax your muscles into letting go. Start with stretching your right leg, pulling slowly on your hip and lower-back muscles. Keep the rest of your body still and limp. Repeat with the left leg.

Stretch your entire left side, starting with your waist, small of back, hip, leg, to the toes. Repeat with the right leg. Then stretch upward on the left side, beginning with your waist, chest, arms, and fingertips. Repeat with your right side.

Now slowly stretch your neck, turning your head to the right side, then to the left. Turn it back to its normal position. Feel the muscle strain draining from your face. Stretch from head to toe. Stretch every muscle in your body.

Breathe deeply and quietly. Listen to the soft signals of your body. Listen to the rhythm of your breath as the cool air enters the nostrils and the warm air leaves the lungs. Listen to your heart beating steadily and quietly.

Talk to your muscles and tell them to relax. Tell your eyelids that they are growing heavy with sleep. Tell your mind to turn off its activity because you are tired.

As the ebbing of tension flows out of muscle after muscle, you will experience a state of weightlessness; you will fall into the depths of deep, sound sleep. Should you wake up in the middle of the night or in the early hours of the morning, don't fight to go back to sleep. A good prescription is to get up and do something that does not require mental exertion, such as reading a light or amusing story, writing a letter, or jotting down notes. Some of your best ideas may come at this time, so don't stifle them.

Here's a helpful suggestion: Invest in a portable tape recorder if you don't have one, and leave it on your night table. Record parts of the relaxation and deep breathing given in this chapter. It is easier to listen to step by step instructions than to read them from a book or while you are trying to quiet your thoughts. Be sure that the recorded voice is soft and soothing to induce tranquility and deep relaxation. Timing is important. It must be slow enough for you to follow each suggestive phase of relaxation.

It was Walter John de la Mare who said that "what the will and reason are powerless to remove, sleep melts like snow in water."

MEDITATION AND MIND CONTROL

For many of us the word "meditation" means something that is practiced by a select few and is associated with formal religions—Eastern or Western. We are not accustomed to thinking of meditation as a practice to be incorporated into the everyday lives of ordinary people. But that is *exactly what this book proposes.* The lives of urban, industralized human beings have become so stress-laden that it is essential for us to find a way of release—a way that offsets the stress but does not involve flight from life.

In recent years there has been a surge of interest in meditation because we are all searching for inner peace. Meditation can give it to us through the greatest creative force in the world—mental suggestion.

Meditation is done with perfect calm. No tension. No excitement. No fantasy. When we know how to enter the depths of the mind, we achieve a heightened awareness of ourselves and increase remarkably the ability to focus our thoughts and eliminate distractions.

How do we go about meditating? There are some basic techniques we can learn to still the mind from its ceaseless wanderings, but they can be used only in a quiet atmosphere with absolutely no interruptions. Therefore, they are best utilized at home, where you have control over the environment. When you become more adept, you will be able to alter your state of consciousness from an active state to a deep, quiet state of reverie. An experienced meditator can fall into deep reverie at any time, even in a disquieting atmosphere. This is a mental skill acquired through disciplined practice.

Meditation should be done in a sitting position to keep your mind from falling into a sleep stage. It is important to be physically free of clothing that binds the body, such as a tight collar or belt; even shoes can prevent the flow of blood. Your spine should rest against the back of a straight chair or armchair, with your hands resting quietly on your lap or the fingers interlocked. Try not to fidget. Concentration will come more easily when your eyes are closed.

CANDLE CONCENTRATION

This simple technique brings about rapid concentration on an object because the bright flame of the candle stimulates nerve centers in the brain and alerts the mind.

Place a lighted candle about two feet away from where you are sitting. Gaze at the candle for 2 or 3 minutes. Then close your eyes and envision the flame. In your mind's eye see the light of the flame. Concentrate steadily on this glowing, orange light. From time to time the flame will disappear. Sometimes it will return with a black halo; at other times the flame will appear elongated. Then it will disappear and reappear. If your concentration is deep, you will be able to recall the image of the flame and hold it longer. This ability increases with daily practice, at least 5 minutes each time.

You will find that when your powers of concentration are heightened, you will be able to narrow the focus of your mental vision of objects, people, or places down to the smallest detail that you would normally never observe.

"Strength of mind," said Alexander Pope, "is exercise, not rest."

NUMERAL CONCENTRATION

This Zen exercise is taught to the novice as one of the first steps to mind control. It helps the mind focus by the mental gymnastics of visualizing numbers in sequence timed with each deep breath. After each number is mentally created, it is stored in the repository of the solar plexus, the network of nerves at the upper part of the abdomen.

Don't be dismayed if you suddenly lose a number while trying to picture it in your mind. Your concentration has gone astray. Gently pull it back and continue.

Take a deep breath with eyes closed and picture the number 10 in your mind. See it clearly written in black.

Exhale and mentally place the number in your solar plexus. Inhale and picture the number 9 in your mind. Again, see it clearly written in black. Then exhale and place it in the solar plexus. Repeat the same process until you have reached number 1.

If you have trouble producing a mental image of the numbers, then write a large example of each in black ink or crayon on a separate card. Concentrate on the number with your eyes sharply focused on the black-ink outline. Then close your eyes and project the image in your mind.

In the second stage of the exercise inhale deeply and picture the number 10 in a glorious, brilliant color, say, red. Exhale and place the red number 10 in your solar plexus. Inhale and picture the number 9. This time see it in a luminous electric blue. Exhale and place it in the solar plexus. Continue to picture subsequent numbers with each breath, giving each one a new color until you have reached the number 1.

Some people are able to picture numbers in colors quite easily, and if their powers of concentration are strong, this exercise will not be difficult for them to achieve. But there are others who have difficulty in creating mental images from a projected thought. It is for these people that the numeral exercise will be most helpful.

This particular exercise seems to create varied influences on the mind. One of my students was able to visualize only round figures mentally, such as 3, 6, 8, and 9. She had trouble with angular numbers, such as 1 and 4. Black was the only color she could picture.

The numeral concentration was the answer to relieving insomnia for an elderly woman with rheumatoid arthritis. "Instead of fighting the pillows," she told me, "I lie still and concentrate on this game of mental gymnastics. By the time I reach number 1, I can't think of anything else but sleep."

A business executive who had been a student of mine for several months remarked with great pleasure that the numeral concentration combined with deep breathing "had made a world of difference in [his] golf game." His muscles usually tensed up during the putting, which made his game erratic, and many of his approach shots fell short of or went past the green. By breathing deeply to release tension, and by concentrating to narrow down his point of focus, his muscles began to respond without the usual jerkiness he fought so hard to conquer. He found the secret to improving the accuracy of his game through the techniques of relaxation and mind control.

The numeral-concentration exercise had a bizarre effect on a middle-aged bachelor, who found it "highly stimulating." He told me with a large grin that it had increased his power of concentration. "I can see the whole thing in technicolor. It's a great ego booster."

"Really? How?" I asked.

"Well, it's like this. First I reverse the procedure. I begin with numeral 1... a sexy gal in a white bathing suit with streaming auburn hair looking at me. Then I imagine two more gals. This time they appear with black wavy hair... and so on until I see all ten of them looking longingly at me!"

I must have appeared stunned by his version of an ancient Zen discipline aimed at developing a calm, orderly mind, for he added quickly: "It might not be the traditional way the Zen masters do it, but it sure works for me!"

THE JOY OF MEDITATION

Now that you have an idea of how to relax physically and, to some degree, control your mind's rambling energies, you will be able to enjoy the art of meditation. Give yourself at least twenty minutes for inner reflection.

Take a deep breath, long and slow, and feel a calming influence surging through your body. Simply sitting still is a symbol of stillness within. Close your eyes and continue to breathe rhythmically and quietly. Your muscles will begin to unwind.

Just sink mentally into a sphere of serenity. Let it happen. Don't try to take your mind by storm and crash the gates of serenity. Be gentle. Coax your mind. If it should jump from one thought to another, let it. Observe its restlessness. Don't control it. Now and then you will enter into brief interludes of retreat and into deeper levels of quietude.

An effective way to eliminate restless thoughts is by picturing your mind as a blackboard. Every time a rambling thought appears, gently erase it with an invisible sponge, leaving the blackboard blank.

Depression comes to all of us. But if we know how to control it, we can rise above it. Whenever dark thoughts enter your mind, take a deep breath and draw into your body the forces of energy, strength, and tranquility. Then exhale and slowly empty all negative thoughts like a gently moving current of water until only the good thoughts remain. This will generate new vigor, bringing peace to your mind.

Be conscious of your deep, quiet breathing and its ability to transform the negative into the positive. Let your mind rest in a climate of serenity. Think of yourself as a vast ocean. The waves that rise and fall are your thoughts, thoughts generated by external elements, like waves moved by soft winds and deep currents. Don't cling to them. They are only fleeting and will change like the waves of the ocean. Use the power of your mind to travel light mentally without extraneous baggage to wear you down. See yourself as a happy, positive person. Positive thinking brings about positive action.

Meditation is cumulative. With each new day of practice your mind will begin to form new patterns of thought control. When you are able to exercise influence over what happens within your body and become deeply relaxed when you want to be, yet alert and poised for action when that is required, you will have achieved a competence that you will never be without. It will sustain you in the most stressful situations of your life. At this level of meditation you will begin to experience a marvelous sense of self-awareness highly intensified yet suffused with calm exhilaration.

When you cultivate your mind to achieve enduring happiness, it will be the kind of happiness that springs from within, fed by creative thoughts and emotions. And as Marcus Aurelius said, "No retreat is more peaceful or less troubled than that encountered by man in his own soul."

Chapter 4

Listen to Your Body Rhythm

Our minds have unbelievable power over our bodies.
—ANDRÉ MAUROIS

The first time I heard the phrase "Listen to your body rhythm" was in Shanghai in the late 1940's when I applied for a secretarial position with an English political writer, John Reid. At ninety he continued to write articles for the *North China Daily News* and other Far Eastern papers. I was in my twenties.

John Reid was a blithe spirit. He bore a strong resemblance to George Bernard Shaw. He had the same sinewy build and wicked wit. The remarkable quality about this man was that he understood the internal rhythms of his body so well that he was able to chart his day and make use of time more effectively than anyone I have ever known.

John Reid's day began at sunrise, when his energy level was at its peak. He did most of his writing in the morning and left the afternoon for reading and correspondence when his energy level dropped. Through mental discipline he was able to catnap at spaced intervals to revitalize his energy, then awaken himself at the exact minute desired. This daily routine was followed up with vigorous deep-breathing exercises. Having witnessed many times how his energy soared after these brief recharges, I asked him in amazement: "How do you do it? You have great mind control —you always seem alert and in top form."

"It's simple," he answered, with a devilish twinkle in his eye.

"Just listen to your body rhythm. It will tell you many revealing things about yourself. You will understand your mood swings, the times when you are up and down, your energy range—its peak and low levels—your appetite changes, the amount of sleep you need, and even your desire for sex!"

John Reid's verve for living surged strongly in his youthful frame. At ninety he looked not a day over sixty. This dashing bachelor still courted the ladies in a debonair style.

One morning I arrived early at his old stucco house to catch up with accumulated typing. Wong, his houseboy, let me in with profuse apologies that *lao hsien shêng* (old gentleman) was not available. He pointed proudly to the courtyard carpeted with velvety grass. Through the French windows I caught a glimpse of this grand old man dressed in a thin black polo shirt and loose, Chinese black cotton trousers tied at the ankles, clothes that gave freedom of movement. His silvery-white hair caught sparks of morning sunlight as he moved with lightness of step and spirit in a spectacular choreography of mind and body in action. He was performing the fluid motions of a yoga exercise known as the Sun Salutation. The spatial patterns demanded a supple, well-trained body. This he had acquired while living in India as a young British officer and had worked hard to preserve it. He had great respect for his body, never abusing it by overeating or drinking. He exercised daily and fasted once a week.

Through years of practice in meditation he learned to focus his attention inward and listen for signals the untrained ear cannot hear and the untrained mind cannot perceive. He could raise or lower his blood pressure, increase his body temperature, and even slow down his heart rate.

Political debates were John Reid's favorite pastime. When tempers flared, he knew exactly how to change the course by a little clowning. He would wiggle his right ear as he held firmly to his point of view or work up beads of perspiration on his face to frighten his opponents. Once, in the midst of a heated debate, he took off his jacket and began to empty the pockets of his trousers when one of his friends shouted in fury: "What tricks are you up to now, John?" In seconds he was standing on his head on the carpeted floor of his living room while still carrying on the debate with witty emphasis.

John Reid was an extraordinary human being in total command of his mind and body, but he is also an example of human potential developed to its highest levels.

The West is just becoming aware of the great benefits of the centuries-old Oriental science of mind and body control. Through years of strict training Yoga and Zen masters have acquired the sensitivity to detect subtle shifts in their physical and emotional rhythms. Yogis are able to alter their bodily processes at will, to produce trance stages, be buried alive, stop the heartbeat, and in general tap into physiological functions thought to be beyond the reach of man's conscious control.

For two centuries medical doctors serving with the British Army or Civil Service in India sent back reports about the Indian yogis who could so regulate their involuntary physiological processes that they could even stop their heartbeats. Most Western scientists have regarded these spectacular adventures in self-control with bemused skepticism, giving them no scientific credence.

In 1926 Yogi Desbandu performed some unusual feats before the Bombay Medical Union. He was able to stop the radial (wrist) and temporal (temple) pulse on both right and left sides at will and stop the beating of his heart intermittently.

In 1956 at the All-India Institute of Mental Health in Bangalore, a frail, forty-eight-year-old yogi, Shri Khrishna Ivengar, stepped into a freshly excavated pit dug by the scientific crew who witnessed this event. With prayer book in hand and chanting quietly, the yogi lit his incense and stepped into the pit, where he lay flat on his back. He was wired with electrical instruments so that his vital functions could be monitored. The pit was filled with dirt and covered with a wooden board. In order to survive, the yogi reduced his metabolism enough to sustain himself on the little air that seeped through the dirt. As the experiment continued, the doctors, psychologists, and medical scientists from the World Health Organization waited anxiously while the monitors registered the yogi's heartbeat, respiration, and other life signals.

When the pit was uncovered after more than nine hours, the yogi was found alert and calm. He rose to his feet, smiled, and waved to the hundreds of spectators who showered him with garlands of flowers. Nonetheless, this extraordinary feat made no great impact in the annals of medical science.

In 1969 Swami* Rama, age forty-two, came to the United States to demonstrate to Western medical scientists the benefits of yogic discipline to the nervous system. He was willing to allow his yogic training of mind and body control to be monitored by the modern technology of medical science. This experiment† took place at the Menninger Foundation in Topeka, Kansas.

The swami showed extraordinary differential control over blood supply in his right hand. He caused two areas a couple of inches apart on the palm of his right hand to change temperature gradually in opposite directions until they showed a temperature difference of about 10° F. The left side of his hand was flushed; the right side had turned ashen grey.

The swami wished to demonstrate the stopping of his heart for three to four minutes. But in order to do this it would be necessary to fast for a couple of days, taking only fluids. However, since the swami had other pressing engagements, Dr. Elmer Green suggested that he stop his heart for just ten seconds. It would be an adequate test.

The swami was wired for the demonstration. Before starting his "inner focusing," he asked that when his heart stopped he be informed over the intercom from the control room by the phrase "That's all." This would signal him not to exceed the allotted time. He explained that he did not want to interfere with the functioning of his "subtle heart."** Then he made a few tries at speeding and slowing his heart and suddenly announced that he was going to "create a shock" and no one should be alarmed. Dr. Green thought the swami meant that he was going to give *himself*

*Spiritual master.

†Voluntary Controls Project: Swami Rama Research Department, The Menninger Foundation, June 6, 1970. Biofeedback for Mind-Body Self-Regulation: Healing and Creativity, Research Department, The Menninger Foundation, October 30, 1971. Researchers of both projects: Elmer E. Green, Ph.D., Alyce M. Green, B.A., E. Dale Walters, M.A., D. W. Ferguson, M.D.

**The yogis call the subtle heart the electrical field that surrounds and interpenetrates the physical heart and determines its functional activities.

the shock, but actually he meant that the doctors and researchers watching the polygraph records in the next room might be shocked by what he was going to do.

After about seventeen seconds of motionless silence the announcement "That's all" was heard over the intercom from the control room. The swami then pulled in his stomach muscles for a few seconds and relaxed. The control room interrupted with the information that the heart record was not what the researchers had expected and that Dr. Green should take a look at it. He did and reported to the swami that the swami's heart rate, instead of dropping to zero, had jumped from about seventy per minute to about three hundred per minute. The swami seemed surprised and bothered. "You know," he told Dr. Green, "that when you stop the heart in this way, it still trembles," using his hand to indicate the fluttering motion. When the swami's cardiograph was examined later by Dr. Marvin Dunne, cardiologist and professor at the Kansas University Medical Center of Kansas City, the phenomenon was described as "atrial flutter," a state in which the heart fires at its maximum rate without blood either filling the chambers properly or the valves working properly. Dr. Dunne, who was not present at the demonstration, asked if the swami had passed out after this dangerous and phenomenal feat. Dr. Green told him that nothing of the sort had happened. Instead he and his colleagues quickly unwired the swami so he could get to his lecture on time!

The medical reports indicate that the atrial flutter actually lasted for an interval of between seventeen and twenty-five seconds. The exact duration could not be determined because when the swami drew in his stomach, the resulting electrical signal from the muscle firing caused the EKG pen to go off the edge of the paper, and within seconds after it returned, the heart rate was normal again. By drawing in his stomach, the swami had established a "solar plexus lock" so his heart condition could be maintained for quite a long time, if desired. In summary, the swami stopped his heart from pumping blood for at least seventeen seconds.

The successful experiment with Swami Rama was encouraging to the researchers at the Menninger Foundation. They looked for more rapid ways to teach people with circulatory ailments to control the flow of blood through their arteries. They combined the self-suggestion and visualization techniques of autogenic training with a powerful new technique known as biofeedback into a system for psychosomatic self-regulation called *autogenic feedback training*.

Autogenic training is a form of mental and physical therapy, leading to self-regulation. It was developed by Johannes Schultz in 1910. By repeating simple autogenic or self-directed phrases slowly and deliberately, a state of deep relaxation can be induced. The phrases reflect such expressions as: I feel quiet . . . I am calm . . . my arms and legs are relaxed . . . my feet are warm . . . my whole body feels quiet. Biofeedback is used to detect physiological signals such as muscle tension, blood pressure, skin temperature, and brain waves. This information is "fed back" to the subject by means of external instruments that register results with a needle on a meter or by sound or light signals. Once the subject learns how to regulate the particular physiological process, he no longer needs to use the biofeedback instrument.

Fifty-seven women and eighteen men were selected to test the effectiveness of temperature training as a treatment for headaches. Sixty-three of them were migraine sufferers, ten had tension headaches, and two had cluster headaches.

The volunteers were given instructions in the use of a "temperature trainer" that indicated the differential temperatures of the mid-forehead and the right index finger. They were also given a typewritten sheet of autogenic phrases. Some of the phrases helped them achieve passive concentration and relaxation of the body, and other phrases focused on the achievement of warmth in the hands. They were asked to commit these phrases to memory. Each volunteer practiced daily with the temperature trainer at home and kept a record of the practice sessions. They learned to increase their hand temperatures, which meant increasing the blood flow to their hands and indicates relaxation. In a short time many of the migraine patients were able to raise their skin temperature by 10 to 20 degrees. More than two-thirds of them ended up with warmer hands and fewer headaches.

The migraine sufferers learned to turn off the pain in their heads by warming their hands through the use of biofeedback coupled with autogenic phrases, and not with external heat.

Another interesting experiment conducted by the same researchers at the Menninger Foundation involved the attempted lowering of muscle tension in twenty-one volunteers. Muscle tension is indicated by an electromyograph (EMG). Electrodes were attached to the skin surface of the right forearm of each volunteer to measure the muscle tension. In most cases even though no visible signs of tension were apparent, the needle on the meter registered a continuous firing of motor fibers. As the volunteers watched these signals, seven of them were able to bring the meter needle down to zero in less than twenty minutes through biofeedback training. One volunteer, the only one who had previous training in yogic meditation, was able to do this phenomenal performance without the EMG feedback. Eleven others achieved low-tension levels with the help of EMG feedback. Three did not succeed at all. They showed signs of strain probably due to the conditions of the experiment.

When conditioning experiments on rats were conducted by Dr. Neal E. Miller at Rockefeller University, they indicated the possibility that if rats can learn to speed up or slow down their heartbeats, raise or lower their blood pressure, and increase or decrease their intestinal contractions—all activities controlled by the autonomic, or involuntary nervous system—then surely humans can learn such control.

"The significant difference in controlling the voluntary and involuntary systems," says Dr. Elmer Green, "is that for the voluntary nervous system it is necessary to use *active volition*, and for the involuntary nervous system, which functions below the level of consciousness, it is necessary to use *passive volition*. This is really detached, effortless volition."

When we can learn to control our visceral organs, we will be able to cross the border that divides voluntary from involuntary functions. This means we will be able to control and regulate our heart rate, blood flow, respiration, digestion, body temperature, metabolism, and other vital functions usually regulated by reflex mechanisms. Yoga and Zen masters have demonstrated scientifically that these controls can be learned.

My Experiences with Biofeedback

Since visceral learning is so closely tied in with yogic techniques of relaxation and mind control, I was eager to experiment with this new science. Essentially it is a teaching method similar to trial-and-error learning. For instance, a person learns to become an expert tennis player by visual and neuromuscular feedback. The player *feels* his arm as he sees the ball move and, if he makes a bad shot, corrects his arm the next time to improve his game. Should he make a good shot, he tries to duplicate it. He is not aware of which muscles are involved in hitting the ball with the racket, but with continued practice he becomes a good tennis player. However, if that person were blindfolded, he could not possibly perfect his game of tennis. Similarly, where the internal organs are concerned, we are in the dark, unable to see the constant changes taking place in our body. Through biofeedback we *can* tune in to our bodily functions. Once we actually see how our heart beats or measure the stress or fear we are under, we will have the necessary information needed to begin controlling our internal organs.

The advantage of using the different electronic machines is that every signal of the brain, muscle tension, and electrical skin response is registered on various meters. In my sessions with Joshua Reynolds at the Stress Transformation Center in New York, I could see immediately how the different meters reacted to the corresponding body responses. The first experiment was to increase the temperature of my right arm. The thermistor of the skin-temperature-feedback instrument was attached to the index finger of my right hand. I started with slow, deep breathing and visualized the blood coursing through my entire body. Then I concentrated on the blood flow in my right arm. It began to feel hot and heavy. As my nervous system relaxed and my blood flowed into my hands and feet, a sense of calm came over me. I closed my eyes and continued to breathe quietly and deeply. In half an hour my hand temperature had increased from 70° F. to 90° F. This skin-temperature measurement is different from our normal internal temperature of 98.6° F. The skin temperature is related to the body's metabolic rate. By relaxing, you lower your metabolic rate, which causes an increase in skin temperature.

In another session I concentrated on muscle relaxation in my face and neck through the EMG (electromyograph) feedback. Electrodes were placed on my frontalis, a muscle of the forehead, to monitor the tension level. I was able to establish contact with my facial muscles by tensing them first, then relaxing them. I could then discriminate between a tense and nontense state. The frontalis usually contracts when we are agitated or tense, although most of us are unaware of this. Other tension points are the eyes and eyelids and the jaw.

First I contracted my forehead to create deep frowns, then stretched it to ease the frown lines. I tightened my jaws as if to gnash my teeth, then I opened my mouth slightly to avoid contact with my upper and lower teeth and to prevent hard swallowing. I closed my eyes tightly to feel the pressure on the eyeballs, and stretched my lids as if smiling with my eyes. I pulled the muscles tautly in my neck, then relaxed them. I breathed deeply and felt a warm sensation as the tension swept down and out of my face during each long phase of exhalation. I became aware that when the activity in the nervous system slows down, the face becomes calmer.

The clicking noise level on the EMG feedback increases in frequency with the amount of tension in the muscles. I was able to lower the click ratio to a very low level—the lower the level, the more subtle the perception and the greater the field of internal awareness.

In another session I experimented with the hemispheric training. This was an exciting adventure as I listened to the two cerebral hemispheres of my brain discharging their signals. The left hemisphere is the rational brain, responsible for language, logic, reason, and thought. It governs most of our behavioral patterns. The right hemisphere, involved in spatial and intuitive thought, is artistic and subjective: dance, crafts, and art are its responsibilities.

Electrodes of the EEG feedback were attached to my forehead and scalp with dampened salt water. I placed my fingers on the right and left hemisphere machines to feel the vibration. By listening to the two hemispheres of the brain discharging their signals independently, I found that about five seconds out of every minute I heard a simultaneous clicking of the two hemispheres. They clicked together in rhythm like sharp "beep" signals. The more I listened to them working in phase, the longer they clicked together.

The purpose of this training is to get the two hemispheres to work in phase which is their natural state. The more the brain is synchronized in harmony, the higher the intensity or voltage. This increases the amplitude levels of the brain cells. As the neurons of the brain become quieter, the frequency of the brain waves becomes slower. As more neurons are joined in this peaceful state called *synchronization,* more of the brain cells become quiet and receptive.

After a few sessions with the hemispheric training I did not need the EEG feedback to determine when the two hemispheres sent out their "beep" signals independently and when they worked in phase. And the quality of my early-morning meditation at home became more profound, as if the brain cells had been amplified. As I centered my mind on the flow of my breath, a new source of inner peace seemed to emerge from the depths of my being. I felt a great internal lift.

By becoming familiar with the four different bands of brain-wave rhythmic patterns, we will have a better understanding of its function. The different rhythms are: *beta, alpha, theta,* and *delta.*

Beta rhythm (highest frequency of brain waves, 14 to 40 cycles per second) is associated with active processes in which action is focused on the outside world: in reading, writing, conversing, or solving a problem.

Alpha rhythm (brain waves register at 7 to 14 cycles per second) is associated with a more inward focused state. Although the mind is alert, it does not concentrate exclusively on external processes, nor is it engaged in logical thinking. It is associated with meditation, daydreaming, ESP, and hypnosis. It is a relaxed, pleasant state of awareness.

Theta rhythm (brain waves register at 4 to 7 cycles per second) is usually associated with an unconscious or a nearly unconscious state, slipping into unawareness or drowsiness. It vibrates at the borderline of sleep and is often accompanied by dreamlike images. People who are able to meditate deeply demonstrate an unusually high percentage of theta waves during periods of deep reverie. This may be man's most creative and problem-solving range. Yoga and Zen masters emphasize the use of breathing exercises, and the meditative states achieved are associated with low-frequency alpha and theta waves.

Delta rhythm (brain waves register at 0 to 3.5 cycles per second) is the fourth frequency band and is associated primarily with deep sleep. Infants spend most of their time in the delta stage.

OVERCOMING MY FEAR OF CATS

When psychologist Thomas Budzynski at the University of Colorado explored the possibilities of combating general anxiety through biofeedback, he was successful. In one remarkable case he was able to cure a twenty-two-year-old girl from more than one phobia, among them fear of heights, fear of crowds, fear of riding in cars, and claustrophobia.

I was eager to test my own psychological block through biofeedback. For most of my life I have been terrified of house cats. I could not control my sense of panic in their presence. I never dreamed I would ever be free of that fear, since I did not want to undergo long sessions of psychoanalysis. It has always remained a mystery to me how this phobia started, for I have no memories of any frightening experiences with cats at any time in my life. Joshua Reynolds suggested I try biofeedback.

During the first session of the experiment the electrodes of the GSR (galvanic skin response) feedback were attached to the index and middle fingers of my right hand, a direct link with the sympathetic nervous system, where emotions are centered. The subject of cats was discussed. Every time the word "cat" was mentioned, the needle on the GSR meter flipped as if I had pushed a panic button. The sound was similar to a blasting siren indicating the depth of my fear. There was a major change in my sweat glands as my fear became evident. The sympathetic nervous system sent impulses to the sweat glands that, in turn, reduced the skin resistance. The needle continued to waver at a fevered pace during the hour-long discussion. After the session I felt quiet and at peace with myself. It was a pleasant evening, so I walked home and forgot all about cats.

I stopped at the little grocery store where I usually shop. The only thing I disliked about that store was the fat gray cat that usually blocked the entrance. Without thinking, I walked into the store. Then I made a quick about-turn and realized that I had not noticed the cat. It was there standing guard as usual. I walked up to it and shook my finger in a foolish gesture. "I'm not afraid of you, silly cat!" I said, overjoyed by my reaction. Though still shaky, I proceeded to shop with one eye on the cat.

After another session of *desensitization,* during which the subject of cats was discussed, the needle on the GSR feedback wavered beyond the quiet response stage, but its tempo was not as frantic. Since my anxiety response to cats is a learned reaction, it can be *unlearned.* Cats create the stimulus of aversion in me, bringing about an "anxiety response," and this can be cured only by a "relaxation response." Developing this is easier said than done. We may have established conditioned responses, which are quite crippling if we allow ourselves to be wholly controlled by our mechanical emotional center. Such responses may relate to a particular food which once made us ill, or to swimming if we once nearly drowned or to driving a car if we have had a bad accident. However, if we are slowly exposed to stimuli that were once traumatic or associated with traumatic experiences, we *can* overcome our conditioned responses and regain our freedom of action. Every time the subject of cats was discussed, for example, the needle on the GSR meter reacted less and less. Obviously I was becoming more relaxed with the subject. Joshua was pleased, and so was I.

My second encounter with a cat was quite unexpected. It happened at a friend's house. As I opened the door to her bedroom to get my overcoat, her Siamese cat leaped from the windowsill toward me. My friend rushed to my aid but I stopped her, much to my surprise. My legs trembled as the cat approached me. I knew I had to face the ordeal of palpitation or fear, which is part of the desensitization process. "It was really not the cat that made me afraid," I tried to assure myself, "but the anticipation of the fear of it." All this logic at such a crucial time helped me through. The cat sniffed, looked up at me, then meandered off. Just as I was ready to leave she walked stealthily toward me. I stood still. My knees became weak. My palms were wet with perspiration, but I did not panic. She mewed, looked up at me, then brushed her tail against my leg. I felt nauseated, then suddenly relieved that I let her touch me.

My third encounter with a cat, a week later, was another surprise. As I opened the door that led to the stairway of a friend's house, her cat was sitting on the step. My heart palpitated with fright and surprise. I broke out into a sweat. Without a moment's hesitation I closed the door, separating the cat from me. No one was at home. My friend was due back in about fifteen minutes. I waited a few seconds, then I said aloud to myself: "This is foolish. I *must* face that cat!" I opened the door. The cat was still sitting on the step. I reached out and stroked it with trembling fingers. But each time I stroked the cat my arm seemed to grow stronger and the caresses were more tender—the way I would lovingly pet a dog. "I can't believe it!" I cried out to the cat. "I'm not a bit afraid of you!" The cat squinted its gray eyes, mewed, and felt quite contented with my stroking. I was jubilant.

Cats did not reappear in my life for several weeks until one day, when I stepped in a crowded elevator, I was face to face with an Angora cat squirming in its owner's arms. It mewed nervously:

"We'll be out soon, kitty," I said as I reached out to stroke the cat.

"She likes you!" the young owner exclaimed.

"Does she? I'm so glad to hear that," I responded with a surge of joyous emotion. My instinct to stroke the cat was not premeditated. I felt like shouting out to all the people in the elevator: "Look! my hand is not trembling. . . . I am stroking a cat!"

Strengthened by this conquest of fear, I headed for the little grocery store to test my reaction to the fat gray cat there that, for years, caused me many moments of utter panic. I found it sprawled out on the floor taking in the afternoon sun. I knelt and stroked it. My hand was strong, without the slightest tremor. The cat promptly sat up and closed its eyes. I reached for its paw and held it. "Nice cat," I said softly. It blinked and strolled off with an independent air.

"You sure like cats, don't you?" the old Italian grocer said to me. "Some of my customers hate my cat. Can you imagine anybody hating this cat?"

There was no point in trying to explain to Mr. Antonio how I overcame my fear of his cat and cats in general. It all happened within a period of some weeks.

I have written about this episode with frankness only to use it as an example of how we can break down our psychological ills, whatever they may be, if we know how to face them. We can do this through the new behavioral science of biofeedback, which reveals to us instantaneous information about our internal processes whether they be physiological or psychological. Though still in the experimental stage, biofeedback applies the scientific technology of the West to the ancient concepts and techniques of traditions from the Middle and Far East. It is no longer a question of one culture being superior to another, but the merging of the two. Many of the esoteric and abstruse concepts of Oriental mind control over perception, cognition, and brain function can now be monitored scientifically.

Biofeedback has already made inroads in the sports world. Twenty-year-old golfer Bradford Reynolds, brother of Joshua Reynolds, became the new Lancaster City-County Amateur Champion in Pennsylvania, defeating the five-year reign of the previous champion with a sudden victory. Reynolds achieved this through an accelerated course in biofeedback. Before the biggest tournament of his life, he worked on relaxing under pressure and on recognizing subtle cues for "staying cool" on the course so that tension would not undermine his game. Then he practiced visualization exercises—how to see each shot and picture the score in his mind. The key was then to let his body follow through naturally. When Bradford was attached to the EMG (electromyograph) feedback, which records very slight changes in the activity of the muscle fiber, he could see his mental images actually bringing about very subtle muscular responses When he was asked to visualize squeezing the club handle, it brought about slight changes in the electrical activity of his forearm muscles as measured by sensitive EMG instruments. Soon Bradford saw how a mental picture of his shot actually programmed his muscles for that imagined shot. "This self-programming," says his brother,

Joshua Reynolds,* "is only effective when the system is relaxed." Bradford learned the art of deep relaxation and the ability to preserve his precious energy, so that he would not uselessly expend his energy through tension, worry, and fear. He won the tournament in a dramatic and exciting manner. After his victory he jubilantly said that his reserve energy, calmness, and ability to concentrate better helped him immeasurably to withstand the grueling pressure of tournament play.

Psychologist Thomas Budzynski is optimistic about the future of biofeedback. He believes there will come a time when doctors will lend patients an EMG machine instead of handing out sleeping pills to calm their nerves. He also foresees a time when corporations will have a cot and an EMG machine to reduce anxiety among high-level executives.

Biofeedback has already brought potentially important understanding to the treatment of a variety of conditions, from migraine to hypertension. Its most significant contribution to medical science is in teaching how to relax the nervous system, the body, the emotions, and the mind. Man's biggest problem in this modern age of increasing complexity is stress. These relaxation skills will enable us to raise our stress threshold.

Someday we may be taught how to control our own symptoms without drugs or surgery. Instead of swallowing pills to calm our nerves or lower our blood pressure, we can now learn to slow down by actually seeing our tensions register on an electronic meter. By observing the needle's fluctiations, we can manipulate our tensions. This may be the key to self-healing capabilities, allowing us to tune in to our bodily functions and eventually control them. It confirms the ancient insight that the only way to become acquainted with the inner self is to develop the ability to look inside. The new tools aid us to comply with that old prescription for wisdom: "Know thyself."

*Readers interested in the study of biofeedback can contact Joshua Reynolds at the Stress Transformation Center, 78 East 79th Street, New York City. This center has the latest biofeedback techniques and learning aids for study and for personal use at home.

Rachel Carr

Charting Your Body Rhythm

The theory of biorhythm is taken seriously by many people. The Swiss have devised a pocket calculator, which, when individually set, will show the owner's off days, when he is accident-prone, forgetful, or in low spirits.

In Japan the Ohmi Railway Company stored in a computer the biorhythm of each of its five hundred drivers. At the beginning of each shift, drivers scheduled to have "bad" days are given a card reminding them to be extra careful. In their first year using biorhythm, 1969, Ohmi's drivers achieved a 50 percent drop in accidents, a downward trend that continued the rest of the year.

By charting your body rhythm you *can* discover important clues to your physical and emotional makeup. You will know when to expect your high and low points, your up and down days, your appetite changes—days when you feel fat or thin—times when you are clumsy and drop things, the amount of sleep you need, and other important biorhythms.

Most of us are so out of touch with ourselves that we don't know what to record in a daily chart. Just keep track of important factors about yourself—the time of day when your energy level is at its peak and when it drops, when you begin to feel drowsy or hungry. A pattern will emerge if you keep a daily chart for three months. You will begin to see pronounced cycles. This will help you plan your activities to best advantage. You can then arrange important meetings or conferences during your "up" periods and leave less important affairs for your "down" periods. If you cannot avoid an important engagement during a down period, you will at least become aware of your emotional state and protect yourself.

A daily body rhythm record is included on pages 146-147 to help you get started.

Chapter 5

Your Muscles and
How They Work

Your body is the baggage you must carry through life. The more
excess baggage, the shorter the trip.
—ARNOLD H. GLASOW

Ballet dancers Margot Fonteyn and Rudolph Nureyev, ice skat-
er Peggy Fleming, swimmer Mark Spitz, and skier Jean-Claude
Killy all have one thing in common: They move with a lightness of
body, each muscle in perfect rhythmic control, ready to execute
the split-second timing that has won them their fame. But the
majority of us who have not developed our bodies to such levels of
physical perfection are not in intimate touch with ourselves. We
are unaware of the way our hundreds of muscles function, and
when one of these muscles is out of balance, we feel the stress and
strain in movement and wonder what has gone wrong. Understanding how our muscles work will bring us in closer touch with
ourselves.

The body gets its support from the bones, which are linked by
bands of elastic, fibrous tissue called ligaments. Those joints that
must move freely, such as the hips, knees, and shoulders, are
flexible. To reduce friction in movement these joints are lined
with cartilage, a smooth tissue, like the bearings in a machine.
When the body is in good working order, the three basic elements
of bone, muscle, and connective tissue all function with perfect
teamwork.

73

The muscles in the body fall under three categories: *skeletal muscles, smooth muscles,* and *cardiac muscle.*

Skeletal muscles are also known as *voluntary muscles* because they move under the control of the will and as *striated muscles* owing to their cross-striped appearance.

The skeletal muscles are responsible for the mobility of our joints. They provide the voluntary and reflex movements when the signal is sent from the brain through the central nervous system to stimulate action. These muscles work in pairs. When one of a pair contracts, the other relaxes. This basic pattern puts the body in motion. Actually, the majority of muscles work in group action.

Smooth muscles are also known as *involuntary muscles* because they are, according to Western science, not under the control of the will. However, in Eastern culture it has been proved by Indian yogis that they have voluntary control over the so-called involuntary muscles.

These smooth or visceral (organ) muscles receive their signals from the autonomic (self-controlled) nervous system. These nerves originate in a different part of the brain. The fibers of smooth muscles are spindle-shaped and are found in the walls of the stomach, intestines, vessels, and glands and also in the iris and eyelids.

The cardiac, or *heart, muscle* is in a class by itself. It is a hollow, muscular pump shaped like a strawberry—no larger than a clenched fist. This amazing muscle, composed of striped fibers joined in a continuous network, receives its signals from the autonomic nervous system. It beats out the steady rhythm of life at a rate of seventy to seventy-five times each minute, resting only a fraction of a second before the next contraction. At each beat of the heart three ounces of blood pass into the circulation. After fifty beats all the blood has been completely recharged with oxygen and has given up its load of carbon dioxide.

The heart muscle needs daily exercise. By stepping up the heart rate, more blood nourishment is pumped to other parts of the body and to its own muscular tissues through the coronary arteries and all their smaller branches. This helps *collateral circulation* which means a richer, more extensive network of blood channels to assure an adequate blood supply to all parts of the heart muscle.

When a heart attack occurs from blockage of an artery, the heart tries to provide collateral circulation to recover from the attack. By increasing the blood supply through exercise, new, small blood vessels and capillaries grow to absorb blood to the area deprived of normal flow. Even if arteries are beginning to clog, exercise may reduce blood-cholesterol levels and accelerate removal of fat.

Here are some startling figures about the heart in action. Each day it pumps the equivalent of 3,000 gallons of blood, which it continuously recycles through some 60,000 miles of blood vessels. In doing so it beats about 100,000 times. Under stress and tension it works even harder. We *can* lighten its burden by learning to relax.

There is never a time when all the muscles are in a quiescent state. It takes energy to move a muscle. When we lift a pencil, turn the head, or carry something, the muscle in action becomes tense. It shortens and tightens as it moves, regardless of weight. The muscle contracts even when you grasp a feather. When the muscle is not in use, it returns to its normal length and relaxes. Exercising is more strenuous. When the muscles are in action, they require more oxygen from the bloodstream.

Muscles exert an influence on our metabolism and on our emotions. Good posture is an expression of strong muscles, whereas poor posture is a sign of weak, underexercised muscles that starve for oxygen from the bloodstream. When muscles are weak and tense, they lose their stretch, suppleness, and resilience. They become tight. Tight muscles create tension. This turns into a vicious circle. Tension prohibits muscular relaxation. A muscle must relax; that is part of its function. A way to work off tension is exercise. It is better to walk than ride a few blocks. Walk briskly, breathe deeply, and enjoy the sensation of body freedom. Let yourself go so that no part of your body is held rigid. Your shoes *must be comfortable.* Keep your toes pointed straight ahead, lifting your knees slightly with every step. As you walk, the heel should take the load, then the weight shifts to the ball of the foot and rolls into the large toe. Let your arms swing freely to start the natural springiness to your walk, bringing all your muscles into action, particularly those of your feet and ankles. Walking is an excellent stimulator of circulation. As the leg muscles constrict, they squeeze the veins and push the blood upward. Try it. It works.

Instead of taking an elevator up three to four flights, climb those stairs unless your doctor forbids it. Take deep, full breaths and relax a moment at each landing.

THE BACK

According to the U. S. Public Health Service, more than 70 million Americans have suffered from backaches at some time in their lives. This is generally attributed to muscles that have become stiff and short because of lack of exercise. The major causes of back pain are weak back and stomach muscles. Soft, flabby muscles can be wrenched easily by a slightly wrong move or twist. If the wrench is severe enough, it can tear or rupture a ligament.

For a better understanding of your spine, take a look at the drawing. The spinal column runs from the head to the buttocks in the form of an S. The curves in the spine act as shock absorbers. It is the ligaments and discs that make the spinal column elastic in structure.

The thirty-three vertebrae in the spine consist of bony rings. In the illustration you will see how these vertebrae are divided from the neck to the coccyx. More than 100,000 nerve fibers run through the spine and out through the openings between the bony vertebrae to the various parts of the body. Half are sensory fibers that convey and distribute impulses from nearly all of the muscles and glands of the body and carry sensations of pain, touch, temperature, and muscle tension; the rest are motor nerves transmitting orders from the brain to the muscles.

Each pair of vertebrae is equipped with cushions called discs. These discs are exposed to different kinds of injury. Some are serious, requiring surgery to fuse the two vertebrae when a disc is crushed, and others are less serious but can cause great pain when the injured disc presses on a nerve. The irritated nerve will in turn throw one of its muscles into a spasm. This can be agonizing if the sciatic nerve is affected.

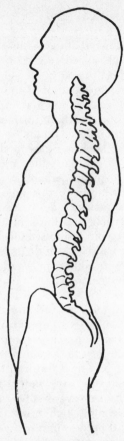

The spinal cord consists of 7 cervical or neck vertebrae, 12 dorsal or thoracic vertebrae, 5 heavy lumbar vertebrae, 5 sacral segments fused together to make the sacrum and 4 small segments fused together to make the coccyx.

Anyone whose back is protected by strong, flexible muscles seldom suffers from back pain and can sustain serious injuries better than those with weak back muscles. The spine should be protected by strengthening the muscles that support it. These are the muscles of the back, stomach, hip flexors, and the hip extensors. Also, by exercising daily, the spine will remain limber through the years.

Medical research has shown that the business executive, whose life is sedentary, has a higher incidence of coronary attacks than the laborer or farmer, whose working life requires considerable physical exertion. People who do a lot of sitting and no exercise are usually the victims of weak abdominal muscles, which easily become slack. These muscles are then unable to carry their portion of the load, which is then thrust on the back muscles. Such an additional load causes the back muscles to slump from fatigue. They become tense and stiff. Finally they rebel by going into a spasm, causing great pain. A major percentage of low-back pain, as most doctors warn, is attributed to this type of muscular deficiency. Here is something you can do to strengthen those muscles. When sitting, every time you think of it, pull the stomach muscles tight and pinch your buttocks together. You will be amazed at what this little exercise can do for you.

If you have a tendency to slump or stand swaybacked, it is because your muscles are weak. Though it may seem to take less muscle power to stand this way, it is the most stressful to the body because it throws other muscles out of kilter.

There is an important muscle complex in your lower back known as the *iliopsoas*. One of the main controllers of posture, it reaches out in many directions—to the spinal column, the pelvis, and the thigh bones. This powerful flexor of the thighs helps to hold the trunk erect. When excessive weight is imposed on this muscle complex, it can cause severe aches and pains—from a backache to a stiff neck. Simply tightening the muscles in the buttocks now and then will help to improve your posture.

You can also prevent other causes of backaches:

1. Avoid lifting heavy loads, for it imposes severe strain on the back. If you must lift a heavy load, bend from the knees and not from the waist.

2. Sleep on a firm bed. If your mattress is soft, place a board under it.

3. Always try to sit in a firm chair with a straight back that won't cause you to slouch.

4. The wrong type of shoes can contribute to back problems: narrow shoes that pinch the feet, high heels that thrust the body

weight forward, and ill-fitting shoes that do not properly support the arches.

5. When your back aches, *rest*. Constant irritation of the muscles will force them into spasms.

Part II

Exercises for Different Parts of the Body

Your back is a large field of stress muscles that lie on either side
of the vertebral column and form a complex group. Those muscles
easily tightened by tension are the three major ones: the
trapezius, at the base of the neck; the *latissimus dorsi,* across the
ribs; and the *deltoid* at the shoulders. These major muscle groups
get an overall toning from the forward motion of the spine and
from arm stretches.

All the exercises given provide a full range of stretches to
strengthen and limber up weak or tight back muscles, bringing
relief to tension in the neck, shoulders, and lower back. When you
lower your head, an additional supply of oxygen invigorates the
brain, waking up the brain cells. It is one way to get rid of a tired
feeling.

You can test the flexibility of your spine and hamstrings in exercises 3 and 4 *without locking your knees.* If you are able to touch
your ankles or the floor in a sitting position or touch your toes from
a standing position, then your spine and hamstrings are in good
shape. But if you should have any difficulty, do these exercises
with caution. Each day bend a little farther down *without forcing
the muscles to go beyond their capabilities.* They will stretch
with practice.

83

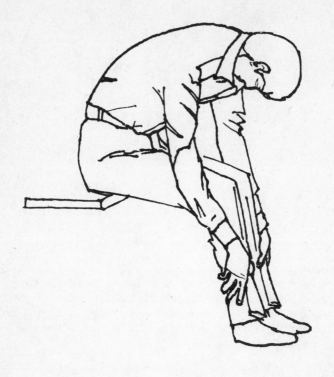

1. Sit and lean forward to grasp your legs *without straining*. Bend only as far as you can. Flex the muscles in your back by gently stretching your arms farther down along the legs. Then slowly pull straight up, using resistance by pitting one muscle against the other. You should feel the stretch in the back muscles. Hold for 5 seconds. Relax. Repeat 5 times. Breathing is free.

2. Sit with legs slightly apart, feet flat on the floor. Clasp
hands, fingers interlocked, with arms stretched back. Inhale
deeply and stretch arms as far back as you can. Exhale and bend
forward with arms straight up, fingers still interlocked. If your
head can touch the knees, let your neck go limp; otherwise just
relax your neck as far down as you can bend. Hold for 5 seconds.
Relax. Repeat 5 times. (With each backward and forward
stretch, extend the muscles a little farther.)

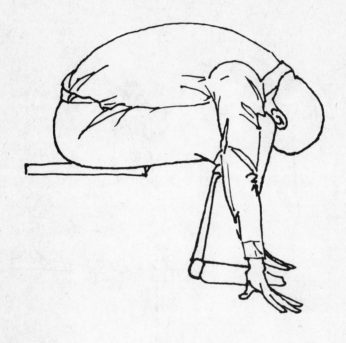

3.   Sit with legs slightly apart, feet flat on the floor. Inhale
deeply, bend down as far as you can with neck limp. If possible,
fingertips or palms should touch the floor. Hold for 5 seconds.
Exhale. Relax. Repeat 5 times.

4. Interlock fingers behind your back. Inhale deeply. As you begin to exhale, bend backward, continue to do so until all the air is expelled. Return to standing position. Inhale deeply again. As you begin to exhale, bend forward, continue until all the air is expelled. Return to standing position. Repeat this dynamic exercise 4 times.

5.   Stand with feet together. Inhale deeply while stretching
your arms over your head. Exhale as you bend down, neck limp.
Stretch only as far as your muscles will allow. If you can touch
the floor with your fingertips or palms, hold for 10 seconds to
feel the complete stretch of the spine and hamstrings. Relax.
Repeat 5 times.

TONING THE BUTTOCKS AND LEGS

The largest and powerful muscle in the body is the *gluteus maximus*—the buttock muscle on which we sit. If this muscle is not regularly exercised, it tends to spread out, as is common in people who sit for long periods of time. Another group of powerful muscles is found in the legs. These muscles should be well exercised to maintain their flexibility and strength.

The play of resistance, pitting one muscle against the other, in the following exercises will help tone and firm the buttocks and leg muscles.

1. Lean slightly forward with feet a few inches apart. Cross arms and place the right hand inside the left knee and the left hand inside the right knee. Then try to press your knees together while pushing them apart with your hands. Hold for 10 seconds. Relax. Repeat 5 times.

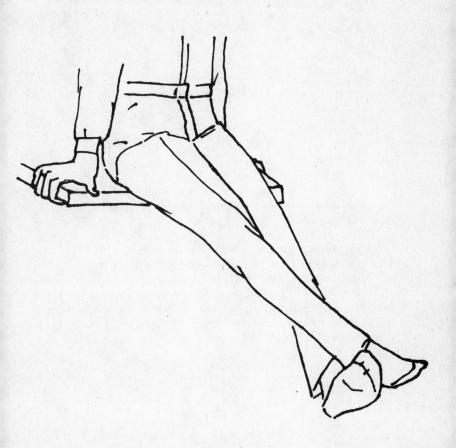

2.   Sit with legs outstretched and crossed at the ankles. Hold on to the seat of your chair. Try to pull your feet apart using resistance. Hold for 10 seconds. Relax. Repeat 5 times.

Rachel Carr

FOR A SLENDER WAISTLINE

Here is an effective way to slenderize your waistline. Be sure that your elbows are not bent and your back is straight. Your posture will also improve.

Stand with feet together. Stretch arms over your head. Interlock the fingers with palms turned up. Inhale deeply while stretching upward (feet flat). Hold your breath. Twist to the right side to feel the stretch along your waistline. Hold for 5 seconds. Then twist to the left; hold again. Stretch upward on tiptoe. Now exhale and relax. Repeat 4 times, alternating right and left sides.

LIMBERING UP SHOULDER JOINTS

The shoulder joints have the widest range of movement of all the joints. When inflamed, they can create great pain that shoots up to the back of the neck and restricts arm movement.

You can get relief with these exercises, which also tone the upper arms. Breathing is free.

1. Stretch arms out to the sides without tensing the neck. Keep stretching as far out as you can. Hold for 5 seconds. You should feel the pull under the arms and in the shoulders and back. Relax. Repeat 10 times.

2. Stretch arms out to the sides, fists clenched, without tensing the neck. Rotate arms in a circle, starting with a small orbit to a large, full one. Make five continuous circles. With each circle, breathe deeply, inhaling and exhaling.

TIGHTENING THE ABDOMEN

Three wide, flat sheets of muscles support the abdominal wall. These are not easy to tone if they have become flabby. It is important to exercise them every day to achieve any results. The ones given here are dynamic and should be done before a meal or at least two hours after eating. Remove or loosen any clothing that binds the waist.

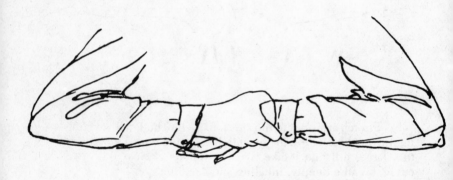

1. Sit with spine straight, feet flat on the floor. Place hands just above the belt, right hand grasping left wrist. With resistance *pull in*, using your arm muscles. At the same time *force out* the abdominal muscles. Hold for 5 seconds. Relax. Repeat 5 times.

2. Sit with spine straight, legs slightly apart, feet flat on the floor. Place hands on the thighs and bend slightly forward. Exhale vigorously through the mouth in a *ha* sound. This will empty the lungs and create a "vacuum" in the abdominal cavity, caving it in. *Without inhaling* (it is not easy at first) forcibly contract abdominal muscles by drawing them up toward the spine, pressing against the rib cage. Hold for 10 seconds *without breathing*. Relax. Repeat 5 times.

When the abdominal muscles have been strengthened through the lift (this may take two to three weeks), exhale in the same way, caving in the abdominal cavity, then rotate the muscles 10 times without stopping. The movement is similar to belly dancing. Relax. Repeat 5 times.

3. The Abdominal Lift can also be done in a standing position, as shown, with the body slightly bent forward.

This is an excellent exercise to improve sluggish elimination of the body's waste products.

IMPROVING POSTURE AND BALANCE

Simple as it may look, it is an excellent balancing exercise to strengthen weak arches and ankles and to improve the posture.

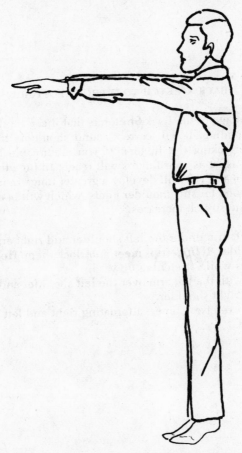

Stand on toes with arms outstretched and together, fingers pointing outward. Inhale deeply and slowly twist to the right. Exhale and twist to the left. Inhale again and twist all the way to the right. Repeat 6 times.

BACK STRETCH TO IMPROVE POSTURE

The advantage of the Back Stretch is that it can be done either sitting or standing. It will correct round shoulders through the pull in interlocking the fingers. If you are unable to do this, stretch only as far as your fingers will reach. In time the muscles will lengthen and you will develop a greater range in movement.

It is also good for stiff shoulder joints, which will become more flexible as the stretch increases.

Place left arm under the left shoulder and right arm over the right shoulder. If fingertips meet, interlock them. Hold for 10 to 15 seconds while stretching upward.

Repeat with the left arm over the left shoulder and right arm under the right shoulder.

Do this exercise 4 times, alternating right and left arms with the stretch.

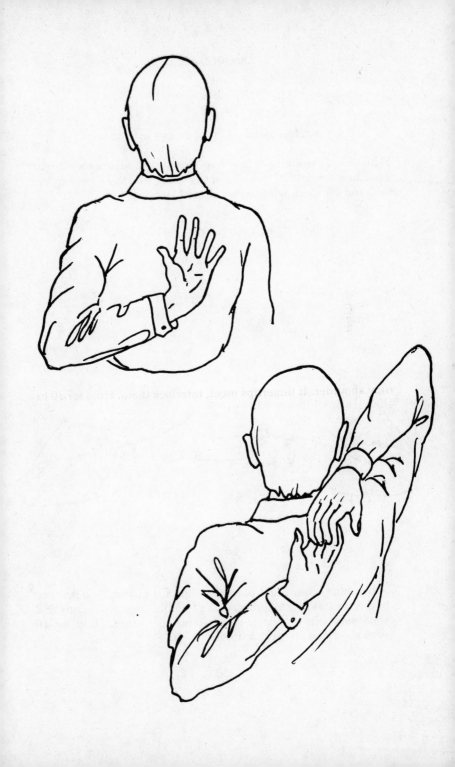

STRENGTHENING THE CHEST AND ARMS

This simple exercise is based on the play of resistance. It will strengthen the deltoid muscles of the shoulders, the biceps in the arms, and the pectoral muscles of the chest.

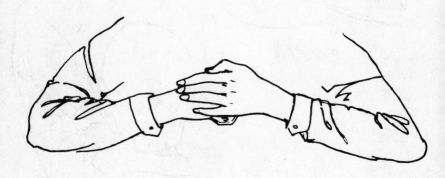

Bend the elbows and place the right fist inside the left, close to the chest. Press together, using forcible strength of arms and shoulders, pitting one muscle against the other. Hold for 10 seconds. Relax. Repeat 5 times.

FOR TIGHT NECK AND SHOULDER MUSCLES

The neck and shoulder muscles are under constant stress, particularly the trapezius muscle, at the base of the neck. This muscle helps to draw the shoulder blades to the spine, raises the shoulders, bends the neck to one side, and turns the face. When it is under attack by tension, try the different exercises given here. They are easy to do and will bring quick relief. The breathing is free.

1. Drop your head limply forward to stretch the back of the neck. Hold for 5 seconds, then let your head drop back to stretch your throat. Hold again for 5 seconds. Repeat 6 times.

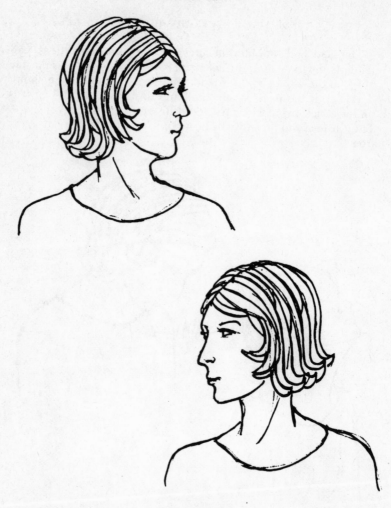

2. Turn your head to the extreme right, looking over the shoulder (without moving the shoulders). Hold for 5 seconds. Then turn your head to the extreme left, looking over the shoulder. Hold for 5 seconds. Relax. Repeat 6 times.

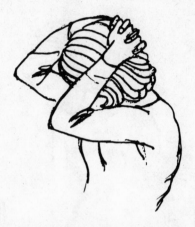

3. Clasp hands behind the head, fingers interlocked. With resistance, pitting one muscle against the other, bring the head forward. You should feel the pull in the upper back and in the neck. Hold for 5 seconds. Relax. Repeat 5 times.

4. Clasp hands behind the head, fingers interlocked. Stretch elbows as far back as possible, bringing the shoulder blades together. Hold for 5 seconds. You should feel the pull in the chest, ribs, shoulder blades, and spine. Relax. Repeat 5 times. (This exercise is also a chest stretch to improve the posture and tone the pectoral muscles.)

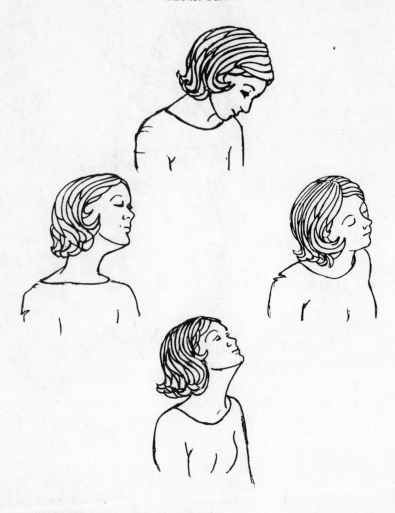

5. Roll your head slowly and loosely in a wide circle. Forward and down, right, back, left, forward. Repeat 5 times. Reverse the motion. The breathing is free, but take a deep breath after you have completed the fifth roll.

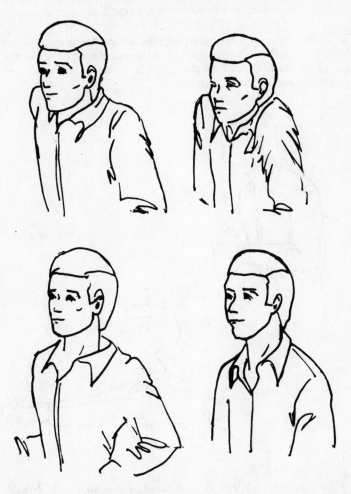

6. Slowly rotate the shoulders in a wide circle: forward, up, back, down (keeping the neck limp). Repeat 10 times. Then raise the shoulders, shrugging them as high as you can. Arch them back to contract shoulder muscles, pulling the shoulder blades sharply together. Hold for 5 seconds. Repeat 10 times.

TONING ARMS AND CHEST, EXERCISING THE LUNGS

These are dynamic exercises that emphasize the play of resistance to tone the arms and chest and at the same time exercise the lungs. *The breath is held for 15 seconds as the movements are repeated 3 times without stopping.*

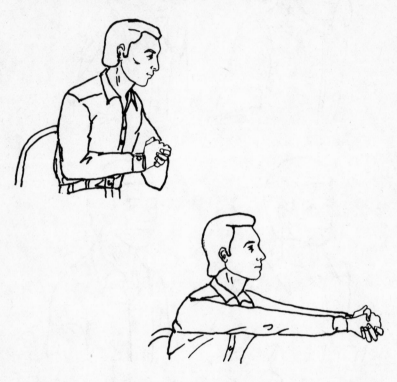

1. *Horizontal stretch.* Clasp hands close to chest. Inhale deeply (expanding the abdomen). Hold the breath as you stretch your arms forward. Use resistance by pitting one muscle against the other to pull the arms toward you, touching the chest. Repeat 3 times without stopping; each movement takes 5 seconds. Exhale and relax.

2. *Vertical stretch.* Clasp hands behind head. Inhale deeply (expanding the abdomen). Hold the breath as you stretch the arms upward. Use resistance to slowly pull the arms down behind your head, touching back of the neck. Repeat 3 times without stopping; each movement takes 5 seconds. Exhale and relax.

TONING THE CHIN LINE

If the muscles along the chin line and neck need toning, these simple exercises will help. They will also prevent premature sagging.

1.   Interlock fingers and place hands on the forehead. With resistance, pitting one muscle against the other, force neck forward. Hold for 10 seconds. Repeat 10 times.

2. Extend your head straight out, stretching your neck as far forward as you can. Shoulders should be relaxed and still. Hold for 10 seconds. Repeat 10 times.

FOR STIFF OR WEAK KNEES

The knees, like the spine, show stiffness with advancing years unless we exercise them regularly. Also, a common injury to the knee joint by sudden twisting or wrenching may result in the detachment of cartilage. This kind of injury can be quite painful and restrict movement. You can increase mobility of your knees with these movements:

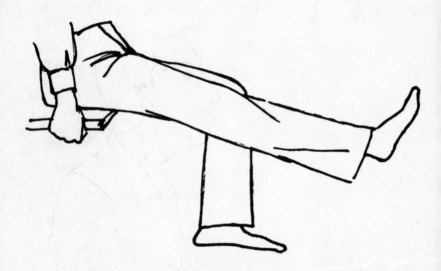

1. Sit in a chair with feet flat on the floor. Hold sides of the chair. Raise the right leg till the knee is straight. Contract the kneecap by pulling the muscles upward, keeping the knee straight. Then press the foot upward, toward you, to stretch back leg muscles. Hold contraction for 15 to 20 seconds. Relax.

2. Move leg backward, under the chair. Contract the knee-cap. Relax. Repeat 10 times with each leg.

3. If you have a weak knee, place a bag of sand (weighing from 5 to 10 pounds, depending on what you can lift) on your ankle and secure it with a string or tape. Lift the leg with this weight. Hold it suspended for 20 seconds. Relax and lower your leg. Repeat 5 times.

4. Deep knee bends are an effective way to limber the knees. Hold on to a doorknob for balance, then bend your knees, back straight, as low as you can. Repeat 15 to 20 times. If you are able to do this exercise without support of a doorknob, then balance with your arms stretched out.

115

FOR TIRED FEET AND WEAK ANKLES

Our feet deserve more attention and care than we give them. So often we wear the wrong type of shoes that constrict the toes, create corns, and chafe the heels. Shoes should be wide and large enough to provide adequate freedom of movement for the feet. When our feet hurt, we hurt all over, causing a backache, headache, or leg cramps.

The two springy arches in the feet are maintained by powerful ligaments, muscles, and tendons that hold the bones in proper alignment. When these arches are weakened, we have what is known as "flat feet" or "fallen arches." The longitudinal arch extends from heel to toe, and the metatarsal arch extends cross-wise in the foot.

An excellent foot and ankle exercise is walking. It should be a natural and easy exercise, but many of us do not find it so. Often the reason lies in the type of shoes we wear.

Here are some exercises to strengthen the arches and ankles and step up circulation in the feet. Do these simple exercises without shoes.

1. As you sit, raise the right foot about 10 inches off the floor. Rotate it slowly with the ankle relaxed—5 times to the right, then 5 times to the left. Lower the leg. Repeat with the left foot.

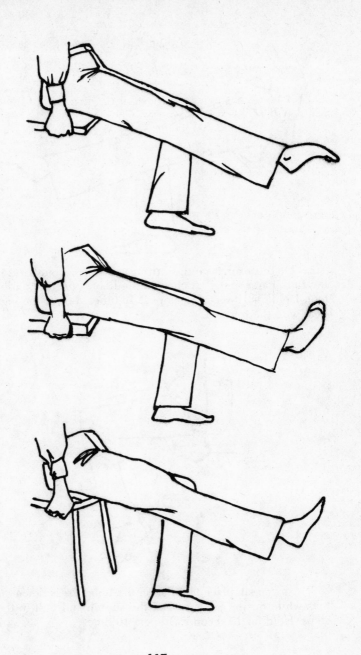

2.   Do this exercise either sitting or lying on your back. Raise the right foot about 10 inches off the floor. Curl toes under the foot. Hold for 10 seconds. Repeat 10 times. Lower the leg. Repeat with the left foot.

3.   As you sit, place feet flat on the floor. Press down on the toes while raising heels to feel the stretch and pull in the insteps. Hold for 10 seconds. Repeat 10 times.

4. Stand with feet together, hands on hips. Rise up on toes. Balance for 5 seconds to feel pull in the arches and ankles. Lower heels. Repeat 10 times. Then rise on toes and slowly rotate feet to outer sides, back on heels, to inner sides, and return to tiptoe position. Repeat 10 times.

FOR PAINFUL, SWOLLEN FINGERS AND WRISTS

The twenty-seven bones in each hand and wrist represent a fourth of the bones in the entire body. Thousands of nerve endings are heavily concentrated in our fingertips. This is why they are extremely sensitive. When our joints are stiff and swollen and our hands don't function as they normally should, we feel paralyzed. The exercises given for release of tension will also help reduce the swelling and increase the range of movement in the fingers and wrists.

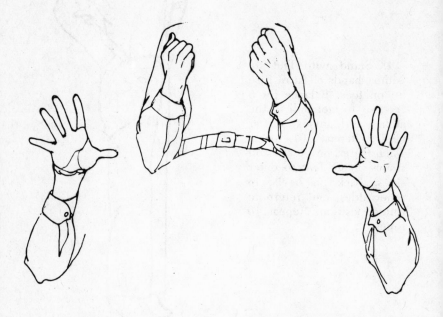

1.   Forcefully spread the fingers apart. Hold for 5 seconds while stretching each finger to its full length and span. Then draw them inward with resistance, pitting one muscle against the other, until you form a fist. Fling them apart again and repeat the same movements 5 times.

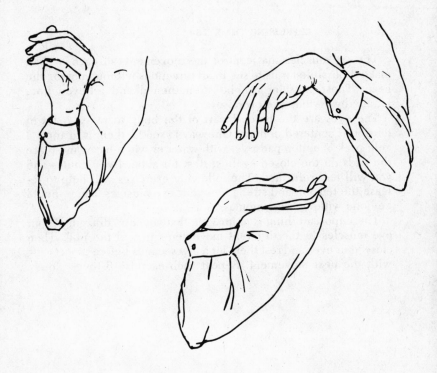

2.   For the wrist, rest elbow on the arm of a chair. With your hand relaxed, slowly rotate the wrist in a circle 5 times to the right, 5 times to the left. Repeat separately with each wrist. Then fling your wrists loosely in circles with your fingers free, as if shaking off drops of water. Do this about 50 times vigorously to increase circulation.

EXERCISING THE EYES

The six muscles that control the movements of each eyeball make it possible for us to see in all directions without moving the head. These muscles can be strengthened and relieved from fatigue by various eye exercises.

The eyes are the hardest part of the body to relax. A lot of tension is centered in them. One way to soothe them is to apply a cold pack of cotton pads wet with water or witch hazel and place the pads on the closed eyelids. Rest for about five minutes and you will feel refreshed. The following exercises will help to release the tension and strengthen your eye muscles. They should be done without wearing glasses.

The important thing is to imagine that you are "dragging" your eye muscles in the different movements to feel the pull. Then close your eyes and rest them for a few seconds before proceeding with the next movement. Repeat each exercise 3 times slowly.

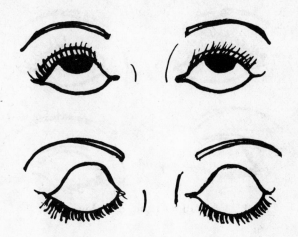

1. Eyes up, eyes down.

2. Eyes right, eyes left.

3. Eyes upper right, eyes lower left.

4. Eyes upper left, eyes lower right.

5.   Eyes in a circle: up, right, down, and left. Reverse rotation.

PALMING

When your eyes are tired after sustained close work, you will find these exercises helpful.

This ancient technique of *palming* to give the eyes complete rest for a few minutes has been used by many eye specialists of today. If it is done properly, it can bring about a calming effect on the mind as well. You should spend at least five minutes resting your eyes.

Bend your head slightly forward, resting your elbows on the arms of a chair or on a desk or table. Briskly rub the heels of the palms together to charge them with static electricity. Cup your hands to cover your eyes, with the heels of the palms resting on the cheekbones and fingers crossed over the forehead. Palms should not touch your eyes.

Close your eyes lightly and imagine a tranquil scene—one that suggests serenity and deep calm. See yourself in the atmosphere of a lake, a brook, a meadow, or any other place that will induce a quiet mental state for you. Try to recall pleasant experiences you have had in any of these places. The longer you will be able to hold this image, the more relaxed you will become.

Let your eyes sink back into a sea of darkness. Breathe deeply and quietly. Then take a long, deep breath and open your eyes. Look around you. Everything will appear suddenly sharper and clearer. This refreshing flash of improved vision will relieve eyestrain and fatigue, at the same time quieting your mind.

CHANGING FOCUS

Change your focus by moving the eyes from a distant point to a closer one. Look at an object as far away as you are able to focus *without your glasses*. Fix your attention on it for 5 seconds. Then move your eyes to a close object, the nearest one you can focus on. Hold your gaze for 5 seconds. Keep changing your focus back and forth 20 times.

Twelve Yoga Exercises to Increase Stamina and Muscular Action

DRAWINGS BY RACHEL CARR

This group of twelve yoga exercises will exert more control over the activity of various parts of your body and are particularly helpful when sustained muscular action is required. They will increase the range of movement and agility of muscles in your spine, hips, knees, and legs.

In the practice of yoga these are the exercises recommended to stimulate sexual activity and increase freedom of physical expression. They are designed to train muscles to work more effectively and efficiently with less mental or physical effort.

It is essential to establish a daily ten-minute routine to get the maximum out of the exercises. They should be done with a minimum of clothing and on a thick rug or exercise mat to allow greater freedom of movement.

129

HIP STRETCH

1. Stand with feet far apart, hands on thighs, spine straight. Turn right foot out; bend knee with right hand resting on it. Stretch left leg away from you till knee is perfectly straight with left hand on side of thigh. Sole of foot must be flat on floor. Inhale and hold for 5 seconds; at the same time press right hand on right knee and contract inner thigh muscles. Exhale; return to standing position, keeping legs apart. Repeat 3 times. Continue same movements bending left knee.

(Limbers hips, firms waist and inner thighs.)

LIMBERING KNEES

2. Sit on floor with legs apart, spine straight, arms to sides. Bend right leg so foot rests on left thigh, heel close to crotch. Grasp right knee with right hand and right ankle with left hand. Gently press knee down to floor or as far as possible without straining. Hold for 5 seconds, release knee, then press down again. Repeat 5 times. Bounce leg slightly to increase circulation. Repeat same movements with left leg.

(Restores elasticity to stiff knees and ankles.)

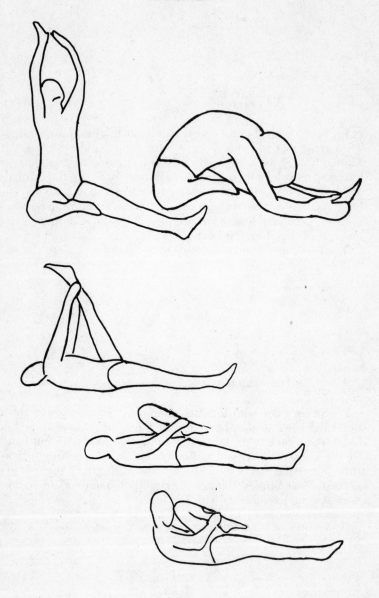

FORWARD BEND

3.   Sit with legs apart. Bend right leg so that foot rests close to inner left thigh. Inhale; raise arms, stretching upward. Exhale; bend forward with head touching left knee (or as far forward as you can reach). Breathe freely and grasp left foot with both hands. Hold for 10 seconds. Then inhale; slowly sit up with arms overhead as before. Exhale; lower arms to sides. Repeat with left leg. Do exercise 4 times.

(Stretches lower-back muscles; hips, legs, and pelvis get a vigorous toning.)

KNEE BEND

4.   Lie flat on back, eyes closed. Inhale while raising left leg straight and high as possible. At the same time bring arms up to grasp left ankle (or as far as you can reach without straining). Right leg remains on floor. Exhale, tightening abdomen while still grasping left leg. Bend leg and bring close to chest. Raise head to meet knee. Breathe freely and hold for 5 seconds. Inhale while slowly lowering head, returning arms to sides and leg to the floor. Exhale. Repeat with right leg. Then continue same movements raising both legs.

(Gives the body an all-around toning and limbering; will help firm abdomen, buttocks, and thighs.)

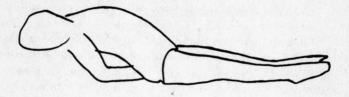

FISH

5. Lie flat on back with legs together, palms down under buttocks, eyes closed. Inhale; raise chest off the floor, using elbows for support to create a bridge between top of head and lower back. While breathing freely, hold pose for a few seconds. Then lower head and chest and slowly return to first position. Repeat 3 times.

(A relaxing exercise, it strenghtens the back and neck muscles. When back is arched, the chest is thrown open for deeper and fuller breathing.)

FIRMING THE ABDOMEN

6. Lie on back with arms to sides, eyes closed. Inhale; raise legs as in diagram, using abdominal muscles rather than strength of shoulders. Hold pose for 20 seconds. Exhale; lower legs and relax. Repeat 3 times. The closer your legs are to the floor the more pull you will feel in the abdominal muscles.

SHOULDERSTAND

7. Lie flat on back, legs together, palms down close to sides. Close your eyes. Inhale while raising legs over head, knees straight, or roll back if you don't have muscular strength to raise legs. Support your back with hands. Breathe freely. Continue to raise legs by pushing hips with hands until legs are in vertical position. Weight of body should be on shoulders and arms, with chin pressing against jugular notch. Keep legs relaxed and together. Breathe freely. No strain should be felt in legs. Hold pose for 20 seconds. If you are unable to get legs up into a vertical position, keep them at an angle as in the previous step. To come down, slowly lower legs by bending your knees, or lower legs without bending them. Let your hands slip farther down along the hips until your back is on the floor with palms down. If you arch your neck back as you straighten the legs, you will be able to keep your head on the floor. Use abdominal muscles when lowering legs to free shoulders from muscular tension. Repeat twice.

(Restorer of youth and vitality. Reverse flow slows down heart rate and calms the nerves.)

Note: If your back muscles are weak and you cannot raise your legs, roll back, using a little momentum so that you can lift your hips.

PLOW

8. Lie flat on back with legs together, arms to sides, palms down, and eyes closed. Inhale; slowly raise legs over the head until toes touch floor or as far as they will reach. Exhale; breathe freely while holding pose for 20 seconds. Continue to breathe freely while slowly returning legs forward. Try to use abdominal muscles rather than strength of shoulders to carry legs forward. Repeat 3 times.

(Massages liver and spleen, limbers up each vertebra to keep spine elastic and elongated, helps tone hips and legs, improves circulation, stimulates internal organs, eases problems of elimination and digestion.)

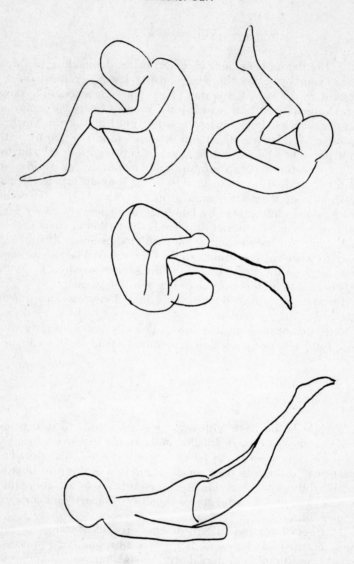

ROCKING THE SPINE

9. Sit with hands clasped under bent knees, head down. Keep back well rounded, knees to forehead. *Fingers remain interlocked throughout the exercise.* Inhale; rock back a little, then exhale and rock forward with head close to knees. Continue to rock back and forth; each time stretch legs a little farther over head until toes touch the floor or as far as they will reach. Repeat rocking motion 10 to 15 times. Then relax completely, breathing quietly and deeply.

(Rapid movements of rocking back and forth are a warm-up to stretch spine and stimulate circulation, causing a surge of energy to flow through the body.)

Note: Don't rush into this exercise if your spine is rigid. Take it gradually.

LOCUST

10. Lie face down, chin on floor, nose up, legs together, eyes closed. Clench fists and place them close together, thumbs touching, under the groin. Inhale deeply. Press fist against floor to thrust legs upward as high as possible keeping head down, knees straight. Hold pose for 5 seconds. If possible, hold breath for this period; otherwise, breathe freely. Exhale; lower legs. Repeat 3 times.

(Helps tone muscles of abdomen and lower back while firming buttocks, hips, and thighs. Holding legs suspended will cause the blood to rush to your face and neck—excellent facial treatment for anyone.)

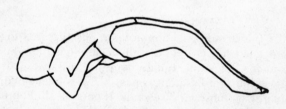

INCLINED PLANE

11. Sit with legs outstretched and together, arms behind with palms resting flat, fingers pointing away from body. With eyes closed, inhale and raise torso. Weight should rest entirely on palms and feet (or heels if you cannot reach that far). While breathing freely, hold pose for 5 seconds. Then lower torso to sitting position with arms behind as before. Repeat 3 times.

(When body is on an inclined plane, there should be no sag in the middle so that the pelvis can be stretched, and arms, hips, back, and thighs strengthened and firmed.)

BRIDGE

12. Lie on back with knees bent. Grasp waist with thumbs up, elbows bent and resting on floor. Inhale; raise buttocks off the floor as high as possible. Keep head on floor without straining the neck. Hold for 10 seconds. Exhale; lower torso and relax. Repeat 3 times.

(Strenghtens lower back and limbers up spine.)

APPENDIX

Notes on Diet

Most doctors will agree that the safe way to lose weight is to follow a well-balanced, high-protein diet. More than 60 million Americans are overweight, and many try to lose the excess poundage through crash diets. This kind of dieting can be extremely dangerous if not carefully supervised by the watchful eye of the physician.

All the energy we get is measured in calories from the food we eat. In addition to calories we require other nutrients, such as minerals and vitamins, to provide good body chemistry. By following a sensible, low-calorie, low-cholesterol diet, we won't be deprived of any essential elements.

Here are some helpful guidelines:

1. Have a medical checkup to determine your correct weight and general health. *This is important.*

2. Keep track of your weight. Whenever you gain a pound or two, take it off before it accumulates. Tuck this fact in the back of your mind: *It takes about 4,000 calories to accumulate a pound of fat, and that pound of fat is harder to lose than to put on.*

3. Eat foods that will satisfy daily needs for proteins, minerals, vitamins, and other nutrients. Most leafy vegetables and fruits, for example, are low in calories and high in minerals and vitamins. Your appetite will be appeased by larger servings of crisp salad greens with a low-calorie dressing at the start of a meal.

4. Avoid fatty, fried foods, gravies, and rich desserts, which overburden the digestive system and may create fatty deposits that block some of the arteries in the heart. Eat broiled or roasted meat, fish, or fowl. A certain amount of fat should be included in every diet. Fat is necessary for the production of bile, which is essential to proper digestion and elimination of waste products. Water is the best purifier to flush out the system.

5. Watching your diet will not keep your body well toned. *Only exercise will do it.*

6. If underweight is a problem, it is best to have a medical checkup to determine the reason. Seek the help of your physician for a prescribed diet to put you on the right track.

DAILY BODY RHYTHM RECORD

Make thirty or more copies of this record and use one each day to note changes in body rhythm. If there is an area of concern that interests you particularly, keep your notes on the questions relevant to your concern.

GENERAL HEALTH

1. Weight before breakfast
2. Elimination: Normal
   Abnormal (state symptom)
3. Any pain or discomfort. If so, state where and when.

APPETITE

1. General appetite during course of the day: Normal
   Increased
   appetite
   No appetite
2. Hunger pangs? If so, when?
3. Any snacks? If so, how many and when?

PHYSICAL ACTIVITY

1. Did you exercise? Specify type
   and period of time:
2. Energy level during the day: High
   Average
   Low

SEXUAL ACTIVITY

Active or inactive.

EMOTIONAL STATE

Did you feel any of these emotional states during the course of the day. If so, when?

1. Mentally alert
2. Mentally dull (easily distracted)
3. Energetic
4. Lethargic
5. Exhilarated
6. Depressed
7. Tense
8. Calm
9. Uncoordinated (clumsy)
10. Coordinated (adroit)
11. Outgoing
12. Withdrawn

HABITS

1. Desire for smoking. If so, how many cigarettes did you smoke during the day and evening before retiring?
2. Desire for alcohol? If so, how many drinks did you have during the day and before retiring?